The Open University

D1189358

Block 4
Slavery and freedom

Bernard Waites

This publication forms part of an Open University course *A200 Exploring History: Medieval to Modern 1400–1900.*. Details of this and other Open University courses can be obtained from the Student Registration and Enquiry Service, The Open University, PO Box 197, Milton Keynes, MK7 6BJ, United Kingdom: tel. +44 (0)870 333 4340, email general-enquiries@open.ac.uk

Alternatively, you may visit the Open University website at http://www.open.ac.uk where you can learn more about the wide range of courses and packs offered at all levels by The Open University.

To purchase a selection of Open University course materials visit http://www.ouw.co.uk, or contact Open University Worldwide, Michael Young Building, Walton Hall, Milton Keynes MK7 6AA, United Kingdom for a brochure. tel. +44 (0)1908 858785; fax +44 (0)1908 858787; email ouwenq@open.ac.uk

The Open University
Walton Hall, Milton Keynes
MK7 6AA

First published 2007

Edited and designed by The Open University.

Typeset by The Open University

Printed in Great Britain by Bell & Bain Ltd., Glasgow

ISBN 978 0 7492 16856

1.2

B/a200_Block4_e1i2_N9780749216856

Mixed Sources
Product group from well-managed forests and other controlled sources
www.fsc.org Cert no. TT-COC-002769
© 1996 Forest Stewardship Council
FSC

The paper used in this publication contains pulp sourced from forests independently certified to the Forest Stewardship Council (FSC) principles and criteria. Chain of custody certification allows the pulp from these forests to be tracked to the end use (see www.fsc-uk.org).

CONTENTS

INTRODUCTION
Bernard Waites

WHAT YOU NEED TO STUDY THIS BLOCK

- Units 13–16
- *Course Guide*
- *Media Guide*
- Anthology documents
- Secondary sources on the A200 website
- DVD 2, *Sugar Dynasty* and *Breaking the Chains*
- TMA 04

Learning outcomes

When you have finished this block you should be able to:

- understand the origins, persistence and overthrow of New World slavery, and the reasons for its racial character

- compare New World slavery with another system of bonded labour: serfdom.

Further, more specific, learning outcomes are given at the beginning of each unit in this block.

INTRODUCTION

'Slavery' and 'freedom' are among the most emotive words in our social and political vocabulary. This block should help you understand why they resonate so powerfully in our culture. So far in A200 you have studied western European history. Now, we turn to the Atlantic 'world' created by European colonisation, transatlantic trade and the forced migration in European vessels of millions of African slaves to plantation colonies in the Caribbean and American mainland.

Slavery was often a punishment inflicted by states on criminals, debtors and convicted rebels, but our concern is with *chattel* slavery, or the ownership of one person by another. In Old English, chattel simply meant cattle; by the seventeenth century, 'chattels' was a legal term for all forms of private property – the goods an individual owned, and which could be sold, bequeathed, mortgaged, given away and seized for debt. Chattel slavery was a social institution permitting the same legally enforceable property rights in people who were invariably outsiders. The most valuable was the right to the slaves' productive labour, which their owners were legally empowered to exact by force. They were also entitled to possess their women slaves sexually, and any child born of a female slave was her master's property. Slavery was therefore a perpetual status for a class of coerced workers; though individual slaves might gain their freedom by self-purchase or manumission, when a master formally relinquished his property right, these did nothing to weaken the institution of slavery as such.

New World[1] or Atlantic slavery was the most extensive, productive and profitable system of chattel slavery in history; it was also unique in being exclusively black.

We will range over more than two centuries and touch on four continents, so the first thing you should do is familiarise yourself with the map of the Atlantic 'world' (Figure 0.1) and the chronology supplied in the *Course Guide*.

The block's written materials are complemented by two television programmes on DVD 2: *Sugar Dynasty* and *Breaking the Chains*. The first affords vivid insights into the wealth and power accumulated by elite slave plantation owners in eighteenth-century Britain, and links most closely to Unit 14. The second dramatises the Jamaican slave rebellion of late December 1831, which proved to be a prelude to the abolition of British colonial slavery in 1834. In Unit 15, you will examine testimony taken from slaves who participated in that rebellion, so the relationship between your written course materials and the television image could scarcely be tighter. Both programmes were made for terrestrial prime-time broadcasting, with budgets that producers of specialist educational television can only dream of. Academic historians advised on the scripts, but the finished programmes exhibit some of the drawbacks of a medium that has to entertain as well as inform. In a short interview on your DVD, Professor Gad Heuman, a leading authority on slavery studies, discusses the programmes with me; what he says should sharpen your critical appreciation of them. How you schedule your viewing will be up to you: *Breaking the Chains* is best viewed in close conjunction with Unit 15, but you can be more flexible with *Sugar Dynasty*. It could be an engaging and informative prelude to the block as a whole. In the DVD notes in the *Media Guide* you will find some background information on the two programmes as well as some questions to bear in mind as you view them, which should prompt your note taking.

---

[1] In this block, I use 'New World' and 'the Americas' interchangeably, and take the Caribbean sea to be part of the Atlantic ocean. I assume the Caribbean islands belong to 'the Americas'.

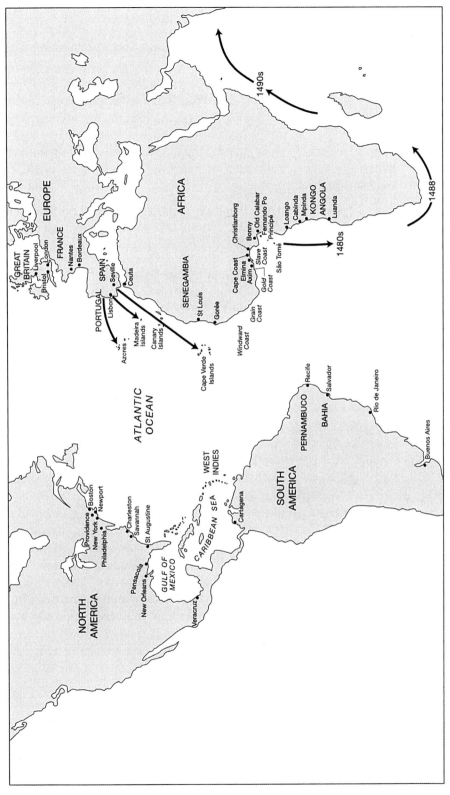

Figure 0.1 The Atlantic world, from James Walvin, *Atlas of Slavery*, Harlow, Pearson Education Ltd, 2006, map 18

Why slavery?

We cannot understand the demographic and moral contours of our own world without some knowledge of New World slavery. Roughly one in three people of African descent were born outside Africa because their ancestors were shipped across the Atlantic as slaves. Black consciousness in the Americas and the Caribbean, and among black Europeans, is rooted in the historical experience of slavery. Modern racism had a viciously circular relationship with black servitude: racist ideologies that deem black people innately inferior can be traced partly to the arguments put forward by whites to justify the enslavement of Africans; conversely, racists found confirmation for what they believed to be the innate inferiority of blacks in the fact that so many endured slavery for so long. In Brazil and the Caribbean, plantation slavery has left a legacy of exhausted soils, dependence on world markets for a narrow range of primary exports and endemic poverty. The demand for restitution is being voiced with increasing frequency: the British parliament handsomely compensated the slave owners when it abolished slavery, but did not vote a penny to recompense the slaves for their unrequited labour and suffering. Radical black voices are now insisting that it is high time this oversight was corrected. Slavery is living history.

Slavery and modernity

Contemporary relevance apart, there is a cogent reason for studying Atlantic slavery in a course that traces the many transformations implied by the phrase 'from medieval to modern': it compels us to ask what we mean by 'modernity'. The word is hard to define in a sentence, or even a library, but at first blush slavery would appear to represent its antithesis. Modern societies prize individual freedom above all other values; it is central to the ideologies of liberal capitalism and democratic socialism. A free labour market is a cornerstone of modern market economies; where slavery persists – as it does in the Sahel states – we take it to be a symptom of socio-economic backwardness. In the broad scope of history, the idea that all are entitled to be free, and that freedom should be embedded in social institutions, is of relatively recent origin. We do not find the concept of freedom as a universal right fully articulated until the eighteenth-century Enlightenment. Slavery, by contrast, is an ancient institution condoned by most civilisations until modern times. Around 1400, although slavery had largely disappeared in northern Europe, it still flourished in the Christian and Muslim Mediterranean. Even north of the Alps, bondage, not freedom, was the norm: most who laboured in the manorial economy were serfs, bound to the land and compelled to render dues to their seignior in labour, kind or money.

The Enlightenment – known in French as *Le siècle des lumières* ('the century of luminaries') – was a pan-European movement of ideas which between c.1680 and c.1780 sought to apply reason, not dogma, to human affairs. Its best-known publicists were French – Voltaire and Dennis Diderot – but its greatest intellects were the German Immanuel Kant and the Scot David Hume. The economist Adam Smith, whose *Inquiry into the Wealth of Nations* (1776) is cited several times in this block, was a key figure in the Scottish Enlightenment and came to enjoy an enormous influence throughout the European intellectual world.

If we identify modernity with individual freedom, how then should we construe New World slavery? Should we see it as an atavism, a throwback to earlier norms, on a par with stoning adulterous women to death in the twenty-first century or teaching creationism as a credible alternative to evolutionary theory? This 'atavistic' interpretation is superficially attractive but very problematic. Scholars usually distinguish between societies that tolerated slavery as a marginal institution and *slave societies* in which the institution dominated economic production and social relationships. There have been only five genuine slave societies: two were in the ancient world, Greece and Rome, and three in the Americas between the sixteenth and nineteenth centuries, Brazil, the Caribbean and the southern states of the USA. It would be straining usage to describe slave societies as atavistic when three out of five originated and flourished in the modern period.

Furthermore, as a system of economic production, New World slavery exhibited several characteristics that we associate with modernity. Technical efficiency was one: sugar and cotton plantations have, for example, been aptly dubbed 'factories in the field' because of the way they coordinated and exploited human labour. But the most salient modern characteristic of Atlantic slavery was 'calculative rationality'. What do we mean by that? Well, whenever economic actors make an investment or buy commodities in bulk to sell to consumer markets, they must calculate future (and therefore uncertain) gains against their original outlay and subsequent expenses (such as shipping and insurance costs). They must also ask whether alternative investments might not be more lucrative, since financial decisions often have 'opportunity costs'. To profit from markets separated by great distances and many months' sailing time, slave traders, plantation owners and colonial merchants had to exhibit calculative rationality in abundance.

SLAVERY AND THE THREE COURSE THEMES

Producers and consumers *[Key thing in Block 4]*

The economic modernity of New World slavery will become still clearer as we tease out the connections with this over-arching theme of A200. Let me offer a stylised account here: over the centuries, slaves performed many social roles in the Old World: they were concubines, domestic servants, harem eunuchs, soldiers and administrators, head carriers as well as productive workers. New World slaves were, in the great majority, *commodity producers* cultivating

[handwritten margin notes: separated by distance / part of the same / commodity market]

export crops (principally sugar) on plantations established solely for that purpose. Most household slaves also lived on plantations. A slave embodied an investment made by a particular type of capitalist: the slave-cum-plantation owner. Slaves were not cheap and the life expectancy of a slave newly arrived in the Americas was relatively short; the slave owner had to calculate whether the expected returns from the slave's lifetime's labour would cover both the slave's purchase price and maintenance costs. Whether to use some of that labour producing the slave's subsistence was another fine calculation: in the Caribbean, the returns from sugar were sometimes so great that it paid slave-owners to import food for their slaves. Coerced labour alone could not be a source of profit: it had to be combined with other factors of production (land, fixed capital) to produce either consumption goods (sugar, tobacco, rice) or industrial inputs into consumer goods (raw cotton). Commodity markets were the nexus between slave producers and European consumers.

Beliefs and ideologies

So far, I have discussed New World slavery in the frigid language of economics. I make no apology for that; its primary purpose was to extract an economic surplus. But it was not 'purely' economic; had it been so, white slaves would have toiled alongside blacks. Europeans had not in the past shown much compunction about enslaving other Europeans; indeed, our word 'slave' is derived from Slav, after the ethnic origins of the Caucasian slaves supplied to the Italian cities by Genoese traders from their colonies on the Black Sea. However, the Europeans who founded American plantation colonies never contemplated enslaving whites, though white indentured workers were employed as field hands in the English and French colonies up to about 1690. The fact that New World slaves were, barring tiny numbers of Native Americans, exclusively coerced black migrants alerts us to the beliefs and ideologies that shaped the plantation system from its inception.

Just as there was no purely economic rationale for black (as opposed to 'colour blind') slavery, so there was no purely economic rationale for abolishing the Atlantic slave trade and emancipating the slaves. Religious belief – notably 'evangelical'[2] Christianity – and intellectual conviction were critically important in persuading British legislators to suppress the slave trade and colonial slavery from above, by changing the law and providing the financial and military resources to enforce anti-slavery policies. The American abolitionists, who sought to abolish the institution of slavery throughout the Union, were in the main evangelical Christians. Beliefs and ideologies are not the entire explanation for the ending of New World slavery: public opinion had

---

[2] The Anglo-American evangelicalism of the later eighteenth and nineteenth centuries had doctrinal affiliations with the evangelical reform movement you studied in Block 2 – especially the doctrine of salvation by faith alone – but also differed in key respects. Perhaps the most important was that, whereas evangelical reform began as a movement *within* the universal Catholic Church, later evangelicalism represented a moral current within Anglicanism and other Protestant sects.

to be mobilised and political coalitions formed; Americans had to resort to a fratricidal war that killed more Americans than any other conflict before their Constitution was amended to outlaw chattel slavery. But beliefs and ideologies are an important part of the explanation, including beliefs that to us are demonstrably false. For example, most economists and many legislators and public officials in Britain came to believe that slave plantation labour was inherently less productive than free labour; this was not true, but it influenced the decision to end colonial slavery in the 1830s.

State formation

Slavery and state formation in the Americas

The relationship of the block to our third theme is, in one respect, straightforward. When the dependent American colonies became sovereign states – usually by rebelling against the imperial power – whether to suppress slavery or tolerate its continued existence was a crucial issue for their new governing elites. Unit 16 gives particular attention to the USA, surely one of the more important instances of sovereign state formation in the modern world. In Spanish America, the patriots who rebelled against Bourbon Spain mostly introduced gradual emancipation measures during the wars of independence. Where slavery was a marginal institution, as in the viceroyalty of La Plata (modern Argentina), emancipation was legislated quite early in the independence struggle (1813 in La Plata). In Mexico, where black slaves were more numerous and economically significant, abolition was delayed until 1829, after independence was secured. Brazil followed a different pattern: it became a sovereign empire in 1822, by agreement with the Portuguese monarchy, and colonial institutions were left undisturbed. Brazil's sugar and coffee plantations continued to depend on African slave imports until 1851, when British naval action and diplomatic pressure ended the Brazilian slave trade. Slavery was not abolished in Brazil until 1888.

Slavery and mercantilist state formation

Before sovereign states were formed in the Americas, colonial slavery had an oblique relationship with the formation of European states and colonial empires through the commercial policies and practices that historians have called 'mercantilism'. Put simply, mercantilism referred to the measures early modern states took to ensure a favourable balance of international trade. They did so in the mistaken belief that a nation's wealth was amassed in gold and silver. Since silver was the medium of international trade, it followed that an unfavourable trade balance drained away silver and so weakened the state's capacity to raise revenue, defend its territory and supply public services. Most states forbad the export of their gold and silver coins and tried to restrict bullion exports. It was recognised that trade between sovereign states could be mutually advantageous: Britain and Portugal, for example, concluded the Methuen Treaty in 1703 by which the Portuguese agreed to admit British woollens and the British agreed to admit Portuguese wines at preferential rates.

But colonial trade was a branch of international commerce in which the state could use its sovereign power to exclude foreigners and to compel its colonists to trade only with the mother country. In the interests of promoting metropolitan economic interests, most states forbad manufacturing and processing in their colonies: sugar could only be exported from the British Caribbean in an unrefined state, for example. The slave trade and plantation slavery were embedded in mercantilist regulations intended to augment the sovereign state's economic power.

The ending of colonial slavery and the dismantling of mercantilist restrictions can be related to a common impulse to liberate economic actors (producers and consumers, buyers, sellers and investors) and to give individuals freedom in their labour, their trade, their getting and spending, their beliefs and opinions.

FREEDOM AND SLAVERY: THE GREAT PARADOX

In this block, you will learn a great deal about slavery and less about freedom. Yet the two were interdependent in the English-speaking Atlantic 'world', where people dedicated to political and personal liberty established exceptionally repressive slave systems, which made servitude a hereditary condition for the great majority of blacks and people of mixed descent. Whereas the Catholic slave codes gave slaves some entitlements under civil and canon law, the Anglophone codes accorded masters an almost unrestricted bundle of rights over their human property. Manumission was less common in the British colonies and the United States; slaves were rarely allowed to purchase their freedom and the children of white men and female slaves usually inherited their mothers' status. Around 1810, free 'people of colour' were about 3 per cent of the total population in Jamaica and the southern USA. In late colonial Brazil, where slaves were able to purchase their liberty and were quite frequently manumitted in masters' wills, free 'people of colour' were a substantial community; in Bahia, the main sugar-growing region, they were about 40 per cent of the population.

The paradox of slavery coexisting with freedom became glaringly evident with the outbreak of the American revolution in 1775. Two months after fighting erupted between American colonists and British forces, the Continental Congress declared: 'We have taken up arms in defence of the freedom that is our birth right, and which we ever enjoyed til the late violation of it ...' (quoted in Degler, 1984, p. 88). When he heard news of the rebellion, the great critic Samuel Johnson mordantly enquired: 'How is it that we hear the loudest *yelps* for liberty among the drivers of Negroes?' (Boswell, 1906 [1791], p. 146). Slavery was a legal institution in all thirteen colonies and their Declaration of Independence was written by a slaveholder. The slaves who made up one-fifth of the population saw the much-vaunted war for liberty as a war to perpetuate servitude; where they could, they fled to the British lines.

The paradox becomes more perplexing when we find the same person advocating both freedom and slavery with unruffled conscience. The most troubling example is John Locke (1632–1704), perhaps the single most important intellectual influence on both the 'Glorious' and American revolutions. From Block 3, you will have gathered that, during the struggles against the absolutist pretensions of the Stuarts, those wishing to restrain monarchical power by representative government argued that freedom is the natural condition of humankind. From 'this state of nature' we all derive certain 'inalienable' rights, meaning they cannot be relinquished in any circumstances. By putting slaves at the mercy of masters, slavery violates the inalienable right to self-preservation; by allowing masters to appropriate the slaves' labour, it violates their right of self-ownership, for we are all entitled to what Locke called 'property in one's own person'. This philosophical doctrine has become embedded in what we now call 'liberalism' (the word was not coined until the 1820s), the most influential ideology in the making of the modern west. The repugnance liberals feel for slavery is evident in the opening page of the fountainhead of political liberalism, Locke's *Two Treatises of Government*:

> The law of nature forbids slavery [which] is so vile and miserable an Estate of man ... that 'tis hardly to be conceived, that an *Englishman*, much less a *Gentleman*, should plead for't.[3]
>
> (Locke, 1967 [1690], p.1)

Yet Locke developed his theory of freedom while deeply implicated in the institutionalisation of slavery in the colonies. In the 1670s, he drafted or helped draft 'The Fundamental Constitutions of Carolina', in which it is stated:

> Every freeman of Carolina shall have absolute power and authority over his negro slaves, of what opinion or religion whatsoever [i.e. irrespective of whether the slaves were baptised Christians].
>
> (Davis, 1970, pp.137-8)

Why a tradition of political freedom was coeval with the practice of black servitude is one of the most challenging questions in British and American history. This block will, I hope, help you understand the paradox of slavery persisting for some two and half centuries in Anglo-American societies where the basic principle of state formation was political liberty.

---

[3] Written around 1680, but not published until 1690, after the 'Glorious Revolution'.

REFERENCES

Blackburn, R. (1997) *The Making of New World Slavery*, New York, Verso.

Boswell, J. (1906 [1791] *The Life of Samuel Johnson, LL.D.*, vol. 2, London, Dent.

Davis, D. B. (1970) *The Problem of Slavery in Western Culture*, London, Pelican.

Degler, C. (1984) *Out of Our Past: forces that shaped modern America*, 3rd edn, London, HarperCollins.

Locke, J. (1967 [1690]) *Two Treatises of Government*, vol. 1, ed. P. Laslett, 2nd edn, Cambridge, Cambridge University Press.

Bernard Waites

> ### Learning outcomes
>
> When you have finished this unit you should be able to:
>
> - understand the global dimensions of the Atlantic slave trade
>
> - understand how the intercontinental market for slaves functioned and how slave prices moved over time
>
> - understand the beliefs and ideologies that legitimated the enslavement of black Africans
>
> - understand the epidemiology and demography of the slave trade
>
> - interpret quantitative data
>
> - appreciate why historians sometimes resort to counter-factual reasoning
>
> - debate the slave trade's impact on African societies.

1415 –
Portuguese took Ceuta

INTRODUCTION

This unit relates closely to the themes of producers and consumers, and beliefs and ideologies.

Before the 1830s, the transatlantic trade in African slaves represented the largest overseas migration in history. For sheer persistence, no other branch of European maritime commerce has rivalled it: the first cargo of slaves shipped directly from Africa to the New World was probably landed on the Spanish Caribbean island of Puerto Rico in 1519; the last shipment of slaves was probably in 1867, to Cuba, which was still a Spanish colony. We will never know precisely how many slaves were embarked on the African coast, and how many were landed in the Americas, during these three and a half centuries. However, thanks to collaborative scholarship, our knowledge of every aspect of the trade has become far more exact in recent decades. Not only do we have a very robust global estimate of the numbers of transported slaves, we also know far more about where and by whom they were bought, how much was paid for them, their destinations and their resale price in the Americas. The first, relatively straightforward, purpose of this unit is to give you an overall sense of these quantifiable dimensions of the trade.

The second, more complex, purpose is to try to explain why a transatlantic trade in African slaves arose at all. I say 'more complex' because explanation is intrinsically more difficult than enumeration, and explaining the human past entails not only saying why such and such happened, but also why certain theoretically plausible alternatives did *not* happen. For example, why didn't European traders purchase European slaves and ship them across the Atlantic? You may feel that understanding what did happen is quite hard enough, without speculating about what did not happen, but so-called counter-factuality can be immensely rewarding in historical enquiry. A transatlantic trade in European slaves is less far-fetched than it sounds, and would have made more economic sense than purchasing slaves on the African coast. Exploring the cultural assumptions that, apparently, prohibited such a trade will give us a better idea of why Europeans opted to purchase enslaved Africans.

This brings me to the third purpose of the unit, which is to assess the demographic and socio-cultural impact of the Atlantic slave trade on the Americas and on Africa. Admittedly, achieving this purpose is fraught with difficulties: with the exception of the English-speaking mainland colonies, the sources with which to reconstruct the demographic history of the Americas are sparse; for sub-Saharan Africa they are virtually non-existent before the colonial era. Why sub-Saharan Africa, a chronically under-populated subcontinent, should have been such an abundant source of slaves for the rest of the world is itself a difficult issue to resolve. Assessing whether participating in the Atlantic slave trade greatly exacerbated the region's demographic fragility is even more problematic. Nevertheless, by making realistic assumptions about Africa's population and its likely rate of growth at the onset of the slave trade, we can use our knowledge of slave exports to assess the trade's long-term demographic impact. Again, the crucial question is counter-factual: what would sub-Saharan Africa's population have been without the continual drain of transatlantic slave exports?

THE OVERALL DIMENSIONS OF THE ATLANTIC SLAVE TRADE

For this section I want you to go to the course website and download and print an article by David Eltis (Eltis, D. 2001, 'The volume and structure of the transatlantic slave trade: a reassessment', *William and Mary Quarterly*, 3rd series, vol. 58, no 1, January, pp. 17–46). The entire issue of this journal was devoted to evaluating the digitalised data on about 27,000 slaving voyages which were published on CD-ROM in 1999 (Eltis *et al.*, 1999) though not, unfortunately, at a price most of us could afford. The database does not include all slaving voyages, but internal checks demonstrate that it captures the great majority. Coverage of eighteenth-century French slaving voyages is virtually complete, and of British voyages only slightly less so. There is, for example, some record for just about every slaving voyage out of Liverpool, the most important British slaving port, and many voyages generated abundant records that have been cross-tabulated. The smaller Dutch and Danish trades are also very well documented.

The major weakness of the database is its imperfect coverage of Portuguese and Portuguese-Brazilian slave trading, although about a quarter of the data relate to Lusophone voyages and it is highly probable that more than half are included. Given the remaining gaps in the evidence, how did Eltis arrive at new global estimates of the trade? With respect to the British, French and northern European trades, where we can be sure that few voyages are omitted, he divided his aggregates by a number which compensated for missing records. Thus, slave departures on Liverpool ships are divided by 0.99, because we can confident that only 1 per cent of voyages from this port went unrecorded. With respect to the Lusophone trade, Eltis reworked previous estimates, using the better-documented data on imports into the English Caribbean as a check on his pre-1700 totals, for which voyage data are sparse. For example, the number of sugar plantation slaves imported into Brazil between 1600 and 1624, when Brazilian sugar exports reached their peak, is most unlikely to have exceeded the 140,000 imports into the English Caribbean between 1640 and 1675, at which latter date sugar exports from the English West Indies surpassed the level of Brazilian exports in 1624. The technology of sugar production in Brazil and the West Indies was identical, so it would have taken the same number of slaves to produce the same amount of sugar.

EXERCISE

I want you to draw a graph which will convey the historical trajectory of the trade. Turn to Table I at the end of Eltis's article and first calculate the annual rate of slave exports by dividing the total in the final column by the number of years to which it refers. Thus, between 1519 and 1600 (which was 81 years) 266,100 slaves were exported, so the annual rate was 3,300 to the nearest decimal point. You can create a graph from an Excel spreadsheet or use a graphing tool, but this is not strictly necessary: a blank sheet of A4, a ruler and a pencil will do. Divide the horizontal axis into quarter centuries and the vertical axis into units of 10,000.

Spend about 30 minutes on this exercise.

DISCUSSION

What should your graph reveal? First, the trade's long, gradual take off: up to the later seventeenth century, the annual flow of exports was no greater than during the post-1850 phase when a considerable international effort was being put into suppressing the trade. Second, demand for slaves reached a plateau in the later eighteenth century: for fifty years, more than 76,000 slaves were exported annually. That is an average figure; in some years, international warfare cut slave exports drastically and in other years they exceeded 100,000, but there was no trend either up or down. Third, the graph should disabuse you of the common misapprehension that the trade rapidly declined after Britain and the USA outlawed it: average annual exports were much higher between 1800 and 1850 than between 1700 and 1750. Slave trading continued as steamers began crossing the Atlantic and the first telegraph cables were being laid between Europe and the Americas.

EXERCISE

Now use the tables in Eltis to answer the following questions:

1   Which national traders carried the largest number of slaves to the Americas?

2   What proportions of total slave shipments were carried in British vessels between 1601 and 1650, and between 1651 and 1700? What does this indicate about the changing pattern of demand for slaves?

3   Spain had the largest land empire ever known in the Americas, which was the most important market for African slaves before 1650, and Spain was a great naval power, yet Spanish vessels shipped scarcely any slaves before the nineteenth century; why was this? (Refer also to p. 23, footnote 25, in the Eltis article.)

4   Which American region received the largest proportion of slaves throughout the trade?

5   Which was the single most important destination for slaves in the later eighteenth century?

6   What were the mortality rates on the 'Middle Passage' during the periods 1601–50, 1701–25 and 1776–1800? What do the figures imply about conditions on slave ships?

7   What proportion of slaves was shipped on British vessels between 1726 and 1800?

8   What was the principal effect of the British/US decision to outlaw the trade in 1807? What do the figures tell us about the British Navy's campaign to suppress the trade? (Look at the 'Africa' column in Part 2 of Table III, which represents the numbers of slaves liberated from slaving vessels and landed mainly in the British colony of Sierra Leone.)

9   What proportion of slave ship shipments came from West Central Africa before 1650 and between 1801 and 1850?

10 Looking at Table III, you will observe that about three times as many slaves were shipped to Jamaica as to British North America (the USA after 1776). Yet (as you will see from the Figure 13.9 later in this unit) the USA had the largest slave population in the Americas by 1825. How can we explain this anomaly?

Spend about 90 minutes on this exercise.

SPECIMEN ANSWER

1   Portuguese or Portuguese-Brazilians shipped the largest number of slaves (over 5 million or 45.9 per cent of the total).

2   British vessels shipped 4.6 per cent of the total across the Atlantic between 1601 and 1650, and 47.8 per cent of *a far greater total* between 1651 and 1700. They increased their market share ten-fold, indicating the extraordinary expansion of sugar production in Barbados and Jamaica.

3   Spanish mainland America imported 57 per cent of slaves disembarked in the New World between 1519 and 1650 (though rather few thereafter). Eltis notes that non-Spaniards could purchase licenses (or *asientos*) to import slaves, which became much sought after by rival European commercial interests.

4   Brazil imported 40.6 per cent of all slaves landed in the Americas, and south-east Brazil was by far the most important single destination over the course of the trade.

5   However, the single most important destination in the later eighteenth century was French St Domingue: between 1751 and 1800 (effectively 1791, because out the outbreak of the rebellion), its total slave imports (593,300) exceeded Jamaica's (586,200) and south-east Brazil's (457,600).

6   The mortality rate on the 'Middle Passage' was the difference in percentage terms between the number of slaves embarked in Africa and the number landed in the Americas. In 1601–50, the mortality rate was 21.4 per cent; in 1701–25, it was 14 per cent; in 1776–1800, it was 10 per cent. The figures imply that conditions on slave ships improved (though it may be that voyage times became shorter, meaning that slaves spent less time in the ships' highly infectious environment).

7   British vessels shipped 40.7 per cent of the total between 1726 and 1800 – by far the largest national 'share' in these decades.

8   The principal effect of British and US abolition was to hand a considerable commercial advantage to Portuguese and Portuguese-Brazilian slavers. It is evident that total slave exports after 1807 declined by much less than the quantities British and American vessels were shipping before abolition. The British naval patrols had only limited effect before 1850: they liberated 91,300 slaves from intercepted slaving vessels between 1826 and 1850, but in the same period 1,398,200 slaves were landed in the Americas (over half in south-east Brazil, which was undergoing its coffee boom).

9   West Central Africa supplied 89 per cent of slave exports before 1650 and 46 per cent between 1801 and 1850.

10 The slave population of the mainland American colonies (or the USA after 1776) grew rapidly by natural increase, unlike that of Jamaica and other Caribbean islands, where the slave population would have declined without continuous imports from Africa. Some slaves reached mainland North America via the intra-American slave trade, but even allowing for indirect imports total slave arrivals there were fewer than 400,000 (see pp. 36–7 of Eltis).

EXERCISE

The text of Eltis's article is quite dense and it is not necessary for you to absorb every detail. Turn to pp. 29–31 and ask yourself whether his 'grand total' of slave departures and arrivals – published in 2001 – is likely to be significantly amended at some future date.

Spend about 10 minutes on this exercise.

SPECIMEN ANSWER

Eltis's total will probably not need to be amended in the future.

DISCUSSION

This is, I know, a hostage to fortune but there are good reasons for believing future estimates will not vary significantly from Eltis's total, which is remarkably close to the estimate arrived at by P. D. Curtin in his seminal *The Atlantic Slave Trade: A Census* (Curtin, 1969). The advance in historical scholarship lies in the accumulation of voyage data, which enables historians to answer a greater range of questions about slaving operations. The overall picture has not been greatly modified in the last thirty-five years; it is the internal details that have become much clearer.

| EXERCISE | What do the observations on pp. 31–2 tell us about the consumer market for imports in Africa? How did this affect slavers' operations? |

Spend no more than a few minutes on this exercise.

| SPECIMEN ANSWER | Africans were discriminating consumers who did not exchange slaves for worthless baubles, and there were sharp regional variations in consumer taste. To achieve economies of scale, and avoid too long a stay on the African coast, slaving captains normally concentrated on a single port of call, to which they often returned on subsequent voyages. The central paragraph on p. 32 makes clear that slave trading was a highly specialised business in which European and African traders were equal parties. |

| EXERCISE | From the discussion of the regional sources of slave supply on pp. 33–5, where would we look in Africa for evidence of slave trade's severest impact on demography and social structures? |

Spend just a few minutes on this exercise.

| SPECIMEN ANSWER | On the evidence of slave exports, the answer is unquestionably West Central Africa, from where slaves were exported via Luanda, Benguela and the Congo (or Zaire) estuary. Except for the late seventeenth, early eighteenth century, it was always the most productive source of slave exports. |

| EXERCISE | In his final paragraph, Eltis emphasises how the examination of the data set requires us to revise the way we normally look at the slave trade; what – according to him – do we need do? |

Spend just a few minutes on this exercise.

| SPECIMEN ANSWER | Stop thinking of Africans as mere victims. African agency influenced the overall supply of slaves, their age and sex profiles, and imposed all kinds of costs on European traders which they would not otherwise have had to meet. |

See also Matthews: 4.2

THE AFRICAN CONTEXT OF THE ATLANTIC SLAVE TRADE

When the Portuguese established regular contacts with sub-Saharan Africa, they found societies much like their own: they had a similar range of pre-industrial crafts, engaged in regular commerce and were usually organised into kingdoms, with a recognised aristocracy or elite. Except where influenced by Islam, Africans did not practise writing, build in stone, use gunpowder or (as far as we know) sail across the oceans. But they were much better equipped to maintain equal relations with Europeans than the indigenous peoples of the Caribbean or the Brazilian littoral. One reason for this is that they had not been biologically isolated from the rest of humanity (as had native Americans) and did not succumb to the devastating epidemics that swept through the American tropics. Moreover, the African disease environment was especially hostile to incomers – a point I will develop further. But it must be stressed that Africans retained the military power to confine Europeans to the coast, where they lived and died on the sufferance of African rulers. When Europeans built their coastal forts, this was normally after an exchange of 'notes' by which they recognised African sovereignty and agreed to pay a rent.

African societies also resembled European in that many of their members lived in various degrees of unfreedom. There was nothing unusual in this: bondage of some sort has been the common lot for most of history. However, sub-Saharan Africa has been unusual in the number of slaves it has exported to other world regions since antiquity. The Muslim conquest of the southern Mediterranean basin in the seventh century, and the establishment by Muslim merchants of regular trade across the Sahara and the Red Sea, gave an added impetus to the external flow of African slaves. Islam forbad the enslavement of Muslims, and imposed a religious duty on masters to convert their slaves (though a period of religious 'apprenticeship' was condoned). As 'people of the book' Christians and Jews had a tolerated place in Islam; they could be held captive for ransom, but were not usually sold as chattels. These precepts were often ignored, but they generally meant that slaves and their children were assimilated into Islamic society over time. On the other hand, there was a constant demand for slaves (not necessarily black) in the Muslim states of North Africa and the Middle East, where they were used as concubines, soldiers, administrators and domestic servants. The fact that slavery – for pagans – was a well-recognised institution, but slaves were not a self-perpetuating class, created a regular demand for imported African slaves. The fragmentary evidence makes calculating the numbers entering the Muslim trades a hazardous matter. One scholar has tentatively estimated that 4,300 slaves a year crossed the Sahara in the fifteenth century and 5,500 a year in the sixteenth, with perhaps half that number leaving annually by the Red Sea and East African coast (Austen, 1979). When the Portuguese made contact with the Guinea states, such as Benin (see Figure 13.1) they were already integrated into Muslim slave-trading networks, and slaves were used locally as porters, to clear the forest and to mine gold. Some of the first slave-trading undertaken by the Portuguese was shipping slaves from one part of the West African coast to another, where they were exchanged for gold.

EXERCISE

It has been argued that these pre-existing Muslim networks facilitated the origins and development of the transatlantic trade because West Africans were already familiarised with slave dealing. Bearing in mind the discussion in the previous section, how significant do you think the 'Muslim factor' was in the development of the transatlantic trade up to 1650? (Refer back to Eltis's Table II.)

Spend about 10 minutes on this exercise.

SPECIMEN ANSWER

Its significance was probably very marginal before the later seventeenth century; until 1650, nine out ten slaves were shipped from *West Central Africa*, a region untouched by Islamic influence. Annual shipments from the whole Guinea coast

POINT TO MAKE
↓
religion
↓
beliefs + ideologies

Figure 13.1   Map of Africa, *c.*1700, showing limits of Muslim influence, principal slave-trading coasts and location of places named in this unit

were less than 600 a year in the sixteenth century, and about 800 a year between 1601 and 1650.

DISCUSSION

The 'Muslim factor' was not irrelevant to the efflorescence of maritime slave trading from West Africa, but its true significance came later, in the early and mid eighteenth century, when combined exports from the Bights of Benin and Biafra, and the Gold Coast much exceeded those from West Central Africa, and English were the main carriers. Muslim traders (known as *slatees*) supplied slaves to Europeans and Luso-Africans based on the coast, but also continued to organise trans-Saharan slave caravans. The 'Muslim factor' had a further importance in that pagans were often enslaved during jihads, or 'holy wars', in the interior, and then channelled to the coast, though again this did not become a significant way of producing slaves until the last third of the eighteenth century.

EXERCISE

It is sometimes asked why Africans sold so many other Africans into slavery, but if you think about it this question is naïve; why?

Spend just a couple of minutes on this exercise.

SPECIMEN ANSWER

Africans did not *know* they were Africans before the twentieth century; this identity usually came from outside, especially from Afro-Americans travelling to Africa.

DISCUSSION

I would add that sub-Saharan Africa has long been the world's most linguistically and culturally heterogeneous region. Social identities were, consequently, highly localised and focused on lineage and a community of ancestors. Household slaves were common in African societies but were rarely sold for export. So-called trade slaves were 'outsiders', usually taken in war or kidnapped by raiding parties. Figures 13.2–13.4 show various aspects of the slave trade in Africa.

Why were powerful Africans, living far beyond the influence of Islam, willing to supply trade slaves? In the academic literature, answers to that question fall into two broad positions:

- powerful Africans were seduced into supplying slaves by an external demand (the Atlantic trade), which led to the institutionalisation of slavery in African societies and the destructive extension of slave trading

- powerful Africans enhanced their wealth and power by adapting pre-existing African institutions to an external demand, which did not radically alter social structures and practices.

POINT TO MAKE

wealth.

Figure 13.2   A coffle or human chain of slaves in the African interior. Photo: Nancy Carter/North Wind Picture Archives

Figure 13.3   Slaves being delivered by canoe to slaving vessels. Reproduced with permission of the Hakluyt Society

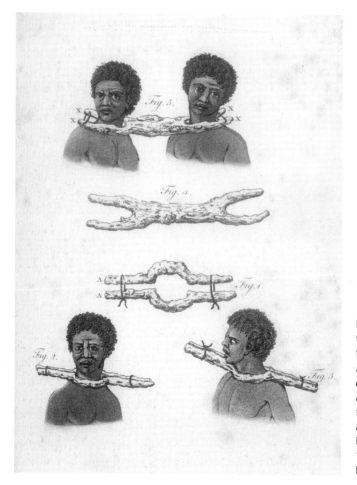

Figure 13.4   Yokes used to collar recalcitrant slaves from Thomas Clarkson, *Letters on the slave-trade, and the state of the natives in those parts of Africa, which are contiguous to Fort St Louis and Goree,* London, James Phillips, 1791. Photo: The British Library

The first was trenchantly argued by the Guyanese Marxist Walter Rodney and popularised in *How Europe Underdeveloped Africa* (Rodney, 1972), one of the most widely read introductions to African history. In brief, Rodney argued that African societies were relatively egalitarian before contact with European slave traders. The basic unit of social organisation was the lineage and, while it included bonded subordinates and coerced dependents, it precluded a sharp division between a class of slaves and slave owners because dependents or their children were incorporated into the lineage over time. According to Rodney, external demand for human labour induced powerful Africans to turn dependents, especially those recently acquired through war, into commodities, which they exchanged for goods that either brought greater prestige (such as sumptuous Indian cottons) or more power (such as firearms and cutlasses). This led, he argued, to vicious and socially debilitating cycles of violence during which powerful Africans systematically raided enemies for slaves. It also, he believed, made the social condition of a 'trade slave' quite distinct from that of a household dependent, and so institutionalised slavery in Africa. Rodney's claims were made within the broader thesis that Europe's pre-colonial commercial relations with Africa systematically 'underdeveloped' the continent by:

- exacerbating technological backwardness (since the availability of slave labour discouraged the adoption of labour-saving technology)
- blocking capitalist development (since there was no inducement to employ wage labour and profit from rising labour productivity)
- fostering political fragmentation.

These were powerful arguments but with respect to the question I asked – why were powerful Africans willing to sell slaves? – the balance of academic opinion has shifted to the second position. Historians are now much more insistent on the primacy of African agency in the slave trade. John Thornton put the case very clearly in *Africa and Africans in the Making of the Atlantic World, 1400–1680*:

> the slave trade ... should not be seen as an 'impact' brought in from outside and functioning as some sort of autonomous factor in African history. Instead, it grew out of and was rationalized by the African societies who participated in it and had complete control over it until the slaves were loaded onto European ships for transfer to Atlantic societies.

> The reason that slavery was widespread in Africa was not ... because Africa was an economically underdeveloped region in which forced labor had not yet been replaced by free labor. Instead, slavery was rooted in deep-seated legal and institutional structures of African societies, and it functioned quite differently from the way it functioned in European societies.

> Slavery was widespread in Atlantic Africa [before contact with Europeans] because slaves were the only form of private, revenue-

producing property recognized in African law. By contrast, in European legal systems, land was the primary form of private, revenue-producing property, and slavery was relatively minor ... [African] slavery was in many ways the functional equivalent of the landlord–tenant relationship in Europe and was perhaps as widespread.

Thus, it was the absence of landed private property – or, to be more precise, it was the corporate ownership of land – that made slavery so pervasive an aspect of African society ... [it] was possibly the most important avenue for private, reproducing wealth available to Africans [and] it is hardly surprising that it should have been so widespread and, moreover, be a good indicator of the most dynamic segments of African society, where private initiative was operating most freely.

(Thornton, 1992, pp. 74, 86)

EXERCISE

We look to evidence to settle historical arguments and, while we have none emanating directly from African societies, we have a fair amount from Europeans with first-hand knowledge of slaving. Much of it was compiled as the abolition movement gathered momentum in Britain in the later 1780s and the trade's impact on African societies became a matter of public controversy. Thomas Clarkson, who led the movement outside parliament, was indefatigable in gathering testimony from men who had served on slaving ships, which he published as *Essay on the Efficiency of Regulation of Abolition* (1789). But the trade's defenders were just as energetic in presenting testimony to support their interests, and found some highly congenial opinions in a series of letters from Sierra Leone by John Matthews, a Royal Navy lieutenant, who served there in 1785–7. (On his return, he was deputed by the Committee of the Liverpool African Merchants to give evidence to the committee of the Privy Council that enquired into the trade in 1788.) Extracts from Clarkson's pamphlet and Matthews's letters are reproduced as Anthology Documents 4.2 and 4.3. Read these documents, summarise their key contentions and say which gives the more persuasive account of the trade's impact on African societies. [Note: the Clarkson material consists of excerpts from his informants' journals; the 'I' is not Clarkson himself.]

Spend about 1 hour on this exercise.

SPECIMEN ANSWER

Matthews's key contention in his letter from Sierra Leone was that slavery was endemic in Africa and that surplus slaves were being incidentally produced by the incessant wars between 'a prodigious number of small independent states' and the routine use of enslavement as a punishment. Had the surplus slaves not been sold to Europeans they would, he maintained, have either died from starvation or been put to death. The claim that Africans in the interior would sell their wives and children for salt (mined in the Sahara) was hearsay, as was his contention that 'Death or slavery were, and still are, the punishments for almost every offence'. His letter from Liverpool was a conscious riposte to the abolition movement. In it, he emphatically denied that wars were undertaken in Africa specifically to acquire slaves or at the instigation of European traders. He noted how jihads in the interior generated a flow of slaves to the coast and was at pains to counter the abolitionists' assertion that the number of offences punishable by slavery in African societies had grown to satisfy the external demand for slaves. Mathews had no direct knowledge of the slave-supply regions in the interior and was relying on information provided by African slave merchants: the 'concurring testimony of many of the most intelligent natives' that jihadists put to death conquered people who refused to convert may have been true, but it was not something Matthews had observed. Nevertheless, Matthews was a persuasive witness who skilfully absolved Europeans from prime responsibility for the slave trade while maintaining that warfare and disruption in African societies preceded the trade and would not have been lessened without it. Though they would be loath to align themselves with Matthews, the views of many modern scholars – such as Thornton – are surprisingly close to his.

The Clarkson material contains first-hand evidence of raids conducted in the Niger Delta and the Cape Palmas region with the express intent of procuring slaves for the Atlantic trade, and more circumstantial evidence of slaving parties in Angola leaving for the interior without any trade goods, with the clear implication that they were raiding (not trading) for captives. But, in one respect, we have to take more on trust: Matthews was a naval lieutenant prepared to put his views to a committee of the Privy Council; Clarkson was publishing extracts from the journals of unnamed informants. That reservation aside, there are no compelling reasons to doubt their testimony.

DISCUSSION

So who was 'right'? Looking at the map of Africa, it is quite possible both sides were: Old Calabar is hundreds, and Angola thousands, of miles from Sierra Leone, and political and cultural conditions varied greatly from region to region. The Muslim presence in the hinterland of Sierra Leone unquestionably brought the jihad into play as a slave-supply mechanism; the Angolan slaving frontier was peculiarly desolate because people migrated inland to escape slaving parties. One conclusion to draw from this exercise is that abolition was not an easy victory for 'progressive' opinion. In refusing to see Africans merely as victims and in stressing that their initiative and enterprise were essential to the trade, today's historians show an affinity with its European defenders rather than its opponents.

EXERCISE

You will have noted from Eltis (p. 38) that nine out of ten slaves were shipped across the Atlantic between the late sixteenth century and 1820 to produce a single commodity: sugar. Given that tropical Africa had abundant land, the right climate and a social institution readily adapted to productive purposes, suggest some possible reasons why Europeans didn't establish sugar plantations there.

Spend just a few minutes on this exercise.

Africa didn't have climate to establish sugar plantations.

SPECIMEN ANSWER

Possible reasons include the following:

1   African soils are comparatively infertile and therefore the American tropics had a distinct ecological advantage.

2   Africa had a hostile disease environment.

3   African agency was effective in confining Europeans to coastal enclaves.

DISCUSSION

While true, the advantage of the American tropics given in reason 1 would not have compensated for higher transport costs had American plantations been competing with African. American plantations would have been more productive per acre, but

American sugar prices had to reflect the costs of shipping slaves to the New World and sugar to Europe. African prices would simply have had to reflect the costs of shipping sugar to Europe.

Reasons 2 and 3 are both true and are not mutually exclusive, but which was more significant? P.D. Curtin first drew attention to the way epidemiology determined the rise of the plantation complex in a 1968 article (Curtin, P.D., 1968, 'Epidemiology and the slave trade', *Political Science Quarterly*, vol. 83, pp. 190–216), which I would encourage you to download from the course website since it is a model analysis of how disease has shaped history, though it is not essential for you to do so. Curtin's originality lay not in discovering new facts about the past but in assembling what was already known into a cogent explanation for an otherwise puzzling forced migration. Europeans were well aware of the risks of setting foot in tropical Africa; how could they not have been? From the personnel records of the Royal African Company, which enjoyed a royal monopoly on English trade with Africa between 1672 and 1713, we know that of every ten men sent to serve in West Africa, six died in the first year, two died in the second through to the seventh year, and only one lived to be discharged in Britain (Curtin, 1990, pp. 39–40). We now understand that endemic yellow fever and the most fatal form of malaria make this environment so dangerous to outsiders. They also imposed an exceptionally high infant mortality on Africans, though adults who had suffered these diseases as children acquired immunities. Unlike Native Americans, Africans had acquired immunities to the commoner diseases of the Asian-Afro-European land mass, and so contact with Europeans did not lead to the devastating epidemics that depopulated the Americas. Moreover, Africans newly arrived in the American tropics had a better chance of survival than newly arrived Europeans. Both died in greater numbers than established residents, but mortality data for the late eighteenth, early nineteenth century show newly arrived young whites dying at about four times the rate of newly arrived Africans of the same age. We now know that this is because Africans had acquired immunities to the prevalent tropical diseases (principally yellow fever[4]) but for a long time the capacity to labour in the tropics was considered a peculiarity of the African 'race'. It is plausible to project this mortality differential back into the mid seventeenth century, when the labour options open to planters were white indentured servants, contracted for three to seven years, and African slaves. Although a slave cost twice as much as indentured servant, he or she was more likely to live longer – and labour for life. Economically, the slave was the more rational choice.

The epidemiological argument remains compelling, but we need to recognise that the disease barrier was not *perceived* as an insurmountable obstacle to African plantations. To Englishmen who could recall the plague carrying off thousands of their countrymen, tropical Africa's environment probably seemed rather more benign than it does to us. Although his colleagues were dying like flies, a Royal African Company factor cheerfully assured head office in 1706 that 'the land about Sera leon (as also elsewhere) is very good & seemingly will bear anything especially ye sugars or Rice plantations'; another wrote home from Cape Coast Castle 'Everything that thrives in ye West Indias will thrive here' (Eltis, 2000, p. 143). All the chartered companies trading in Africa – Portuguese, English, French, Dutch and

---

[4] Yellow fever was probably introduced into the Caribbean around 1520 with the first direct shipments of slaves from Africa.

Danish – entertained schemes to impose control on African production. What stopped these pipedreams becoming realities – over and above the horrendous disease mortality – was the Europeans' inability to extend their military and political power beyond their coastal forts, where they depended on local goodwill for food, fresh water, sex and other services. There was no escaping the constraints of African agency.

Africans in charge

THE EUROPEAN CONTEXT OF THE ATLANTIC SLAVE TRADE

Beliefs and ideologies

Early modern Europeans had little compunction about working other Europeans to death in *punitive* slavery. Tens, perhaps hundreds, of thousands convicted of non-capital offences were condemned for life to Mediterranean galley slavery. Such was the demand for galley labour that German states regularly sold convicted criminals to Mediterranean ports. Irish and Catholic rebels defeated in the seventeenth-century British civil wars were sold as slaves to Barbadian planters. The poor who could but did not labour were stigmatised and criminalised throughout Europe: convicted vagrants could be whipped, mutilated and forced to work in houses of correction. For the labouring poor, notions of civil liberty were selective, even in the more liberal states: British sailors were kidnapped by state agents and forced into the Royal Navy. Until the later eighteenth century, Scottish miners were serfs; when a mine changed hands, they were sold along with the winding gear and mineral rights. So why were white Europeans not sold as chattel slaves? A European slave trade would, we may surmise, have made more economic sense.

Why not European slaves?

There is no single, obvious answer to that question. Rather, we have to refer to a backdrop of cultural assumptions which in the later Middle Ages had led, at least in northern Europe, to all white Christians being included within an implicit communityof those who could not be bought and sold as slaves, however barbarously they might be treated in other ways. The distinction between punitive and chattel slavery had become very clear in law and custom, and the latter had virtually disappeared from northern Europe by about 1400. The enslavement of defeated enemies was sanctioned by the Roman 'law of nations' but this could justify neither the enslavement of the king's peaceful subjects, nor slavery being a hereditary condition for people who, in natural law, were regarded as 'born free'. The basis of this implicit community was ethnicity rather than religion: Catholicism and orthodoxy had condoned slavery for a millennium and more. Theologians could cite unambiguous scriptural authority for hereditary slavery for 'outsiders', which many saw as punishment for original sin. Baptism did not redeem a black skin from slavery.

Before they began to ship Africans across the Atlantic in great numbers, Europeans entertained various beliefs and prejudices as to why black people

European views on "blacks"

should not be part of their implicit community. Their bible was the most authoritative source for all belief; in Genesis, they found an account both of humankind's common origins but also of ethnic differences within the human family, which could be traced to the sons of Noah. Ham was the second son who saw his drunken father, naked and asleep. When Noah awoke and realised his humiliation, he cursed, not Ham, but Ham's son Canaan: 'a servant of servants shall he be unto his brethren'. Where the Canaanites multiplied – and note they were denizens of Sodom and Gomorrah, among other unsavoury places – then 'These are the sons of Ham, after their families, in their tongues, and in their *nations*' (Genesis, 9 and 10, my emphasis). The translators of the King James Bible used 'nation' insistently in Genesis: it conveyed the idea of where you were born and from whom you were descended; the closest modern usage would be ethnicity. The Bible does not say that the 'nations' of Ham are black, but the genealogies and apocryphal interpolations imply that they migrated into lands, notably Ethiopia, which indubitably came to be inhabited by black people. The dark skinned were often referred to as Hamites or Chamites, who bore the curse of Canaan. Although to us cursing children for the sins of their fathers is a monstrous injustice, it was taken as God's inscrutable purpose if you believed the Bible is his word and reveals his mind. So its literal reading could sanction the notion that black people were divinely ordained for perpetual servitude.

The rediscovery of the classical heritage allowed Europeans to link religious dogma to an intellectual rationale for black slavery. Aristotle had asserted that barbarians were slaves by nature and conceived of slavery as the natural relationship of superior and inferior within a household, qualitatively the same as the natural relation of father to child, man to wife, mind to body. The rational basis for slavery lay in the slave's innate, natural inferiority. Aristotle did not say that black people were naturally inferior, and therefore slavish, but blacks had no writing, and indulged in barbarous practices such as polygamy, human sacrifice and selling their own people as slaves. The reclamation of Aristotle's thought encouraged Europeans to pin the idea that some were slaves by nature onto Africans or Hamites.

This is not to say that a racist, quasi-Aristotelian rationale for black slavery had been elaborated before the great acceleration of the trade in the late seventeenth century. Such a rationale was to come later, in the writings of men like Edward Long, the historian of Jamaica, who appears in *Sugar Dynasty* on DVD 2. But there was a clustering of beliefs and ideologies that made black servitude untroubling for white Europeans.

Commercial organisation

Let us turn from beliefs to the business history of slave trading, which reflected broader changes in the commercial organisation of early modern capitalism. Around 1650, the leading players were national chartered corporations with a monopoly on the Africa trade and on purchasing and shipping African slaves to their respective colonies. Mercantilist states delegated sovereign powers to these companies: they could enter treaties with African potentates, build forts to protect themselves against other Europeans, and even wage war. The companies maintained factors, slave-holding pens and small military establishments on the African coast, and conducted what was called 'castle trade'. The British monopoly was transferred from an earlier chartered company to the Royal African Company in 1672 and was supposed to last for a thousand years. But 'private' interlopers were coming into the trade by 1690, and the monopoly was formally ended in 1698 when the trade was opened to all merchants in the British Empire on payment to the company of a 10 per cent duty on exports to Africa. This Ten Per Cent Act expired in 1712 when the last remnant of crown control of Britain's Africa trade ended. The company retained responsibility for its forts and factories in the Gambia and along the Gold Coast and Slave Coast (for which it received a state subsidy) but henceforth the African trade was an open market dominated by private merchants. When the company was chartered, the value of African commodity exports (principally gold) had been roughly equal to the value of slave exports. As the move to private trade gathered momentum, the relative value of African commodity exports declined: the Africa trade became virtually synonymous with the slave trade.

Elsewhere, the shift from monopoly trade to competitive trading by private partnerships came rather later. In France, the slave trade was opened to independent merchants in 1716, with the exception of trade with the colonial ports of St Louis and Gorée (see Figure 13.1), where the chartered Compagnie du Sénégal retained its monopoly for most of the eighteenth century. In both countries, the great majority of slaving partnerships owned the vessel as well as the cargo. Occasionally, a slaving partnership would have a resident factor on the African coast, but more usually they employed a 'supercargo' aboard the slaving vessel to oversee the transactions and protect their interests. Private slavers engaged in 'coasting trade', although, as you will have gathered from Eltis, they usually concentrated on one port of call. Slaving captains worked on commission, which was typically a percentage of the slave cargo. French business partnerships were almost invariably family based and, from around 1750, the leading slavers were predominantly from Protestant and Jewish families, based in Nantes and Le Havre. The most successful were among the richest families in the realm, able to buy prestigious public offices and patents of nobility (Stein, 1979, p. 188).

One of the intriguing findings from the slave-trade database is that, both during the monopoly period and after the switch to wholly private trade, British ships carried 50 per cent more slaves per ton and twice as many slaves per crew member as did their French counterparts (Eltis, 2000, p. 123) (see Figures 13.5 and 13.6). This gave British slavers a considerable competitive edge because shipping costs (made up of sailors' wages and subsistence, the captain's commission, insurance and capital replacement costs) accounted for about three-quarters of the final price of a slave. Delivering European and Asian exports to Africa doubled their price on the African coast, and delivering slaves to the Americas doubled their price. Behind the splendid productivity record of British vessels lay incalculable misery, since the conditions endured by slaves on the Middle Passage were far more wretched than those imposed on convicts. A slave ship carried three times as many coerced passengers as a convict ship of comparable tonnage. Voyages from Africa to the Americas averaged about three months; had they lasted a year, and sustained the same mortality rates, they would have been as lethal to the slaves and crew as the Black Death.

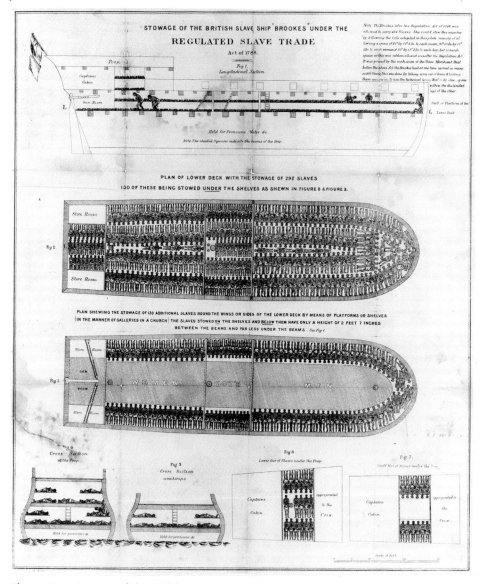

Figure 13.5 *Stowage of the British slave ship* Brookes *under the regulated slave trade act of 1788, broadside, c. 1790. Photo: Library of Congress. The infamous conditions on British slaving vessels were publicised in 1788 by the abolitionist movement when it circulated the plan of* The Brookes. *We can compare this with the plan of the French slave ship* L'Aurore *(Figure 13.6), drawn about the same time. Interestingly, there seems to have been more space to reach the slaves on* L'Aurore; *whether this was because the French drawing was more realistic – as some have suggested – or whether* The Brookes *really did fill every inch with slaves is a moot point.*

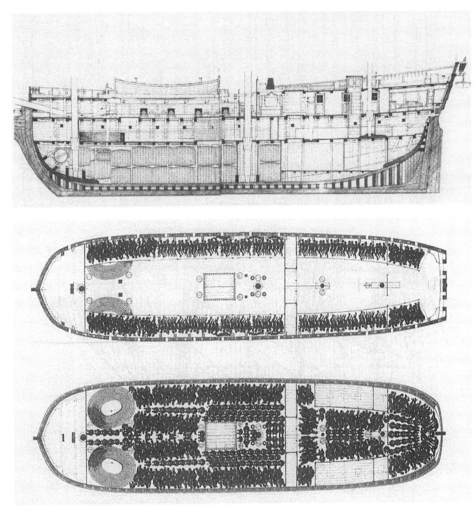

Figure 13.6 Plan of the French slave ship *L'Aurore*. Reproduced with permission of Archéologie Navale Classique Recherche Édition (ANCRE)

EXERCISE

Using Table 13.1, write a paragraph summarising the changes in the geographic location of the British end of the trade; how would you account for them?

Table 13.1 Clearances of slave ships from British ports, 1699–1807

	London	Bristol	Liverpool	Newport	Other (includes colonial ports)	Total
1699–1729	1,595	586	173	12	217	2,583
1730–1749	363	644	553	118	134	1,812
1750–1779	869	624	1,949	358	456	4,256
1780–1807	524	251	2,524	–	153	3,452
1699–1807	3,351	2,105	5,199	488	960	12,103

(Source: derived from Richardson, 1998, p. 446)

In the early eighteenth century, the British trade was predominantly in the hands of London-based merchants, but after 1730 it shifted to west of England ports, presumably because they had a geographic advantage. Vessels sailing out of London were often delayed by adverse winds in the English Channel, and so took longer to reach Africa. Bristol was briefly the most important slaving port, but around 1750 it was overtaken by Liverpool, from which the great majority of slaving vessels departed in the trade's final decades. The reasons for the shift to the Mersey are not wholly clear, but proximity to Lancashire's nascent cotton industry may have been a factor, since textiles were normally the major item in a ship's cargo.

London's financial community was vital in furnishing credit at the outset of the trade and continued to have this role even after its relocation to Bristol and Liverpool. The planters or planters' agents who bought slaves in the Americas very rarely did so for cash; they signed a bill of exchange in favour of their slave suppliers, which would mature in twelve to twenty-four months, and which London finance houses would guarantee (for a discount). This bill would return to, say, Liverpool, where the slaving partnership used it to settle accounts with *their* suppliers, or re-invested it in further voyages. The planter honoured his debt to the London finance house when his sugar harvest was marketed in Britain, and so obtained further credit. London merchants were also major suppliers of the trade goods supplied on credit to Bristol and Liverpool slavers, partly because London remained the hub of the more lucrative East India trade. Indian textiles and cowrie shells – which were used as money in West Africa – were important in the Africa trade's export schedule, probably constituting more than a quarter of exports by value in the 1780s.

A commercial system so dependent on medium-term credit required the legal state to impose stiff penalties on those defaulting on their bonds. Until the 1730s, debt recovery in the British slave empire was hampered by the contradictory interests of two jurisdictions: the colonial assemblies were planter-dominated and sought, therefore, a legal regime favourable to debtors. London and provincial merchants were represented in the Westminster parliament, so it was more sympathetic to creditors. The crucial bone of contention between the jurisdictions was whether real estate and fixed capital could be seized in payment of a planter's debt or whether, as in Brazil and the French colonies, these productive assets were protected against seizure. (A Brazilian or French creditor foreclosing on an indebted planter could seize his harvest, money and personal effects, but not his land and mill, nor his slaves.) The metropolitan merchants eventually persuaded parliament to pass the Colonial Debts Act of 1732, which imposed a uniform debt regime on the British American colonies, and declared that the 'lands, houses, chattels, and slaves' of colonial debtors were liable for the satisfaction of debts 'in the like Manner as Real Estates are by the Law of England liable to Satisfaction of Debts due by Bond or other Specialty' (quoted in Price, 1991, p. 309). When the law was passed, sugar prices were at an all-time low, and many planters were in financial trouble. The law gave metropolitan merchants the confidence they needed to extend their credit operations and, though bitterly denounced by colonial planters, benefited them in the long run. The English-speaking

Atlantic developed credit networks of unrivalled efficiency, which gave planters access to far more working capital than was available to planters in other slave empires. The law also underlined the negation of the slaves' human rights: since they could be seized and sold in satisfaction of their owners' debts, it gave legal sanction to the break up of slave families (which was forbidden under the French *Code Noir* or slave code).

The trade had solid social foundations because its risks and profits were spread among many partners and investors. It was not, as in France, the business of exclusive family networks. A core of ship owners emerged who managed the trade, while 'passive' investors provided much of the working capital. The British trade's capital threshold was *comparatively* low, since slave ships were smaller than in other national trades and voyages were cheaper to fit out. The annual returns on slave-trading voyages after about 1750 averaged around 8–10 per cent, which was higher than in domestic commerce, but the risks were much greater: a slave cargo could be wiped out by disease; ship-board revolts were not uncommon; ships could be seized by privateers in time of war. And with voyages taking up to eighteen months to complete, there was a delay in realising one's investment. Nevertheless, capital was raised without any apparent difficulty: about £200,000 was invested annually in the Liverpool slave trade around 1750 and probably more than £1 million in 1800.

We noted earlier that slave trading on the African coast had to conform to the regional preferences of African consumers, so cargoes varied somewhat between national trades and even ports. Portuguese slavers invariably traded directly between Brazil and Africa, so Brazilian produce – roll tobacco and *aguardente*, a sugar brandy – made up a significant proportion of their shipments. Similarly, when Rhode Island slavers entered the trade, they specialised in shipping rum. But British and French traders tended to ship similar cargoes of mixed manufactures in which textiles were the largest single item. Textiles represented 59 per cent by value of all goods shipped to Africa from France in 1775 and 64 per cent in 1788, but nearly all these cloth exports were produced in India – a telling reflection of economic globalisation in this era. The next most important item in the French export schedule was brandy, which constituted about 10 per cent of exports (Klein, 1990, p. 291). Although the Asian component was exceptionally high in France's Africa trade, the relative weights of its exports was representative of all Atlantic trade with Africa.

Whether the trade was as socially destructive as its critics claimed is debatable. Much turns on the frequency with which the exchange of guns and gunpowder for slaves exacerbated cycles of social violence. During the 1780s – the trade's peak decade – guns and gunpowder were less than 10 per cent of imports by value (Eltis, 1991). Knowing the price of guns, and making heroic assumptions about western Africa's population, we can hazard that one gun per 118 persons was being imported, which suggests they had a restricted role in diffusing social violence. Undeniably, enslavement was a violent process, but many kidnappers and coffle guards were armed with traditional weapons.

[handwritten margin note: rewards + risks]

AFRICAN TERMS OF TRADE

The 'terms of trade' is a key concept in analysing international exchange; it refers to the purchasing power of a country's exports in relation to its imports. If you are unfamiliar with the concept, the following example should clarify it. Textile imports into Africa became relatively cheaper in the early nineteenth century because of productivity gains in the industrialising world. African merchants could command more imported cloth for a slave or a barrel of palm oil in 1820 than they could in 1800, and more in 1840 than they could in 1820. In other words, African terms of trade (or, to be more precise, *net barter terms of trade*) improved because of changes in the comparative costs of production. It would have made economic sense for African entrepreneurs to have switched capital and labour out of producing cloth, and into producing slaves and palm oil, where they had a comparative advantage.

This example conflicts with most impressions of trade between industrialised (or industrialising) economies and producers in the non-industrialised world, particularly the tropical world. With some justice, we think that producers of cane sugar, coffee, cocoa, etc., get a poor return for their exports, so as concerned consumers we buy 'Fair Trade' goods in an effort to improve their terms of trade. Did African slave 'producers' receive a 'fair price' for their slaves? Morally, this is an absurd question. Even economically it doesn't make much sense, since the social costs of exporting Africa's scarcest productive asset must, in the long run, have wiped out private gains. By selling labour, powerful Africans made their societies, and themselves, poorer. But in the objective analysis of the slave market system it is a highly pertinent question. Establishing the secular trends (long-term upward or downward trends) in the purchasing power of slave providers will tell us whether the trade was led by demand or supply, and may help explain its persistence.

The best source for constructing a series of slave prices in Africa is the value of the goods exchanged for slaves when ships were loaded at European ports. Excise officials valued their cargoes and from their records we can establish the *prime cost* of the average slave. I say 'prime cost' because we are dealing with 'free on board' values. The actual cost of a slave purchase included the costs of transporting the trade goods to Africa and insuring them in transit. In the British case, eighteenth-century excise records were kept in 'official' values, based on prices prevailing in 1696–1700, which diverged from market prices as the century progressed. In effect, they are in constant prices which indicate trends in volume rather than the actual prices of British exports to Africa. This can be useful in gauging changes in African barter terms of trade, but to estimate prime costs in British market prices 'official' values need adjusting for inflation.

Using the method I have outlined, David Richardson constructed a price series for slaves purchased in Africa by British traders in Africa between 1699 and 1807. He calculated that the prime price of an average slave rose from about £5 in 1698 to £29–£35 in money terms by the 1800s, and from £5 to £23–£29 in real terms (i.e. adjusted for inflation). However, prices did not increase steadily over time: they fluctuated between £4 and £6 up to 1740, rose gently to about £7 in the next two decades, and then doubled between the 1760s and outbreak of the American War of Independence (1775–83). After being checked by the war, prices rose again in the later 1780s, reached a plateau in the early 1790s, and then surged ahead in the final years of the British trade (Richardson, 1991, p. 33). These price movements are represented by indices in Table 13.2, in which three-year averages are given at selected points in time to smooth out year-by-year irregularities.

Table 13.2   Indices of constant and current slave prices in Africa

	Constant prices	Current prices
1700	100	100
1724/5/6	107.35	99.47
1749/50/51	111.47	97.8
1774/5/6	260.13	260.1
1799/1800/01	389.63	488.53
1806	552.5	678.3

(Source: derived from Richardson, 1991)

EXERCISE

Using the data in Table 13.2, and the preceding discussion, summarise in a sentence or two the changes in African terms of trade over the eighteenth century. What light do the data shed on relations between demand and supply? What was happening in the years immediately preceding the act to abolish the trade?

Spend about 15 minutes on this exercise.

SPECIMEN ANSWER

African terms of trade improved slightly in the first half of the eighteenth century and dramatically in the second. The data indicate that, before 1750, Europeans did not need to raise prices very much in order to expand the supply of slaves: some 2,269,000 were sold over fifty years at static prices in money terms, though African slave suppliers gained somewhat from price deflation in Britain. Over the next fifty years, 3,826,000 slaves were sold (a 69 per cent increase in supply) but real prices rose more than three-and-a-half-fold to elicit this supply and money prices nearly five-fold. In other words, supply became less elastic as the volume of slave exports rose. The material inducements to export slaves had to be stepped up, with the implication that coercion within Africa rose to unprecedented levels. Prices apparently became really high in the 1800s, as planters sought to replenish their stock while the trade was still legal.

DISCUSSION

From Table 13.3, you will see that Richardson's price series correlates closely with price movements for slaves in Jamaica. Given that most of the African coast was an open market, we can be sure other national traders were paying the high prices demanded in the final years of the British trade. The St Domingue revolution and the French decree of 1794 abolishing slavery (listed in the chronology in the *Course Guide*) removed one competitor for slaves, but the British faced others: US slavers were rushing to stock up while federal law still permitted slave imports; Spanish slavers were beginning to supply the Cuban sugar planters; the Portuguese were servicing Brazil's resurgent plantations. With St Domingue in ruins, Brazil's sugar exports soared in the 1790s and 1800s, while planters also invested in a new slave crop, namely cotton. Between 1798 and 1807, about 60,000 African slaves arrived at Salvador in Bahia (Schwartz, 1987, p. 351). African slave entrepreneurs dominated a seller's market: to project back onto this market our contemporary notions of 'unfair' trade, or to see the trade as a species of economic imperialism, would be mistaken.

Table 13.3   Current prices of slaves in Africa and the Caribbean: 1700–1806

	Average current price of a slave in Africa (£) (5-year moving average, except 1806)	Average current price of a prime male slave sold in Jamaica (£) (5-year moving average, except 1806)
1701	5.1	24
1725	5.7	24
1750	6.4	32.6
1775	15.2	49
1800	27.3	78.7
1806	41.1	82.9

(Sources: Richardson, 1991; Eltis and Richardson, 2004)

THE DEMOGRAPHIC CONSEQUENCES OF THE SLAVE TRADE IN THE NEW WORLD AND AFRICA

Demography and labour in the New World

The European discovery and conquest of the Americas triggered the most momentous demographic upheavals in history. The population declined precipitously in the densely populated highlands and was virtually annihilated in the lowland tropics. Apart from 500 or so Caribs in Dominica, who mostly possess West African genes through interbreeding with escaped slaves, and a few people of predominantly native descent in Cuba and Puerto Rico, nothing now remains of the indigenous Caribbean peoples (Watts, 1987, p. 41). Native Brazilians fared almost as badly, and with them died one potential labour supply.

The migratory response to this demographic catastrophe was unique in the history of human migrations for two reasons: first, before 1820, four out of every five migrants to the Americas were either slaves or indentured servants and so sailed with the expectation of being in some form of servitude after the voyage; second, the great majority came not from the continent and states that had seized political control of the New World, but from Africa. Three out every four people who migrated across the Atlantic before 1820 were African slaves. At the slave trade's apogee, between 1760 and 1820, the ratio of African to European migrants was almost six to one; the influx of *permanent* white migrants did not surpass slave imports until 1840. For this reason, Afro-Americans have deeper historical roots in the modern United States than do white Americans: the median date for the arrival of the ancestors of present-day black US citizens was about 1770; the median date for the arrival of the ancestors of present-day Euro-America citizens was about 1900 (Curtin, 1990, p. 109). Prior to the great European migrations of the mid and later nineteenth century, nothing could be more mistaken than the ideological association between the New World and Europeans striving for freedom.

In Britain, we can be forgiven for making that association because English-speaking peoples had an exceptional propensity to migrate during the seventeenth century – when political liberties were being fiercely contested – and the colonies they founded in temperate North America were the world's freest political communities, though one must add 'for whites'. But temperate North America was not the focus of European expansion in the New World. Europeans located most of their capital, and concentrated most labour (whether native or imported), first in the mining economies of Mexico and Peru, and then in the plantation economies of the tropical and subtropical lowlands. The temperate New England colonies were an economic backwater, where the net worth of free white people was, on average, only a quarter of the net worth of whites in the colonies of the upper and lower south. The New England colonists secured a modest prosperity only when they began producing food and other supplies for the plantation islands; by about 1760, three-quarters of their exports were going to the British West Indies (Solow, 1991a, p. 30). The most rapid development in the thirteen colonies occurred where an export crop could be produced by coerced labour. Initially, this had been tobacco, grown by white indentured workers. But tobacco was also being grown in Europe (including England), and the Virginia planters only came to dominate the market by turning to black slaves. Supplementary slave-grown exports were rice and indigo, mainly from Carolina. However, around 1770, the exports of a few West Indian islands were worth more than the total exports of the mainland colonies *combined*, despite their abundant fertile land, their forests of valuable timber and navigable rivers, their herds of European cattle and horses, and their fecund white settlers (see Table 13.4).

Table 13.4   The annual average exports of British North America, 1768–72

	Total exports (£m)	Percentage produced by slave labour	Percentage exported to slave colonies
West Indies	3,910.6	Nearly 100	
Upper south	1,046.9	*c*.50	
Lower south	551.9	*c*.75	
Middle colonies	526.5		42
New England	439.1		78
Total	6,475.0		

(Source: Solow, 1991a, p. 29)

Figure 13.7   The thirteen mainland colonies in 1776

Whatever jurisdiction they were under, the tropical and sub-tropical plantation economies only prospered through the 'blackening' of the labour force and the intensification of servitude (see Table 13.5). Black slaves came to greatly outnumber whites and freed people and their labour-force participation rate was the highest the world has known in peacetime. In western societies, the paid employment of married women and mothers – itself a comparatively recent phenomenon – has been counter-balanced by withdrawing children, adolescents and young adults from the labour force. New World slave populations had very few 'economic dependents', with virtually none of the age and gender differences evident among the free. African women were set to tasks rarely undertaken by white women, certainly in north-western Europe. Planters quickly suppressed any culturally bound scruples about deploying female slaves outside the household and were gender blind when organising whip-driven gang labour. The proportion of children who could not be made to work was also low, partly because male slave imports exceeded female by a ratio of about three to two, but chiefly because of devastating infant mortality. The labour productivity of New World slave populations – or the amount of marketable produce produced per person per year – far outstripped non-slave populations in Europe.

Table 13.5   Slaves, whites and freed people in New World populations at selected dates

	White	Freed	Slave	Slave : white ratio
Barbados, 1690	20,000	–	60,000	3.00 : 1
Barbados, 1833	12,797	6,584	80,861	6.32 : 1
Jamaica, 1698	7,400	–	40,000	5.41 : 1
Jamaica, 1834	15,000	35,000	310,000	20.67 : 1
St Domingue, 1681	4,336	–	2,312	0.53 : 1
St Domingue, 1791	30,381	24,000	480,000	15.8 : 1
Cuba, 1774	96,440	30,847	44,333	0.46 : 1
Cuba, 1827	311,051	106,494	286,942	0.92 : 1
USA, 1780	2,204,949	28,771	546,649	0.25 : 1
USA, 1830	12,858,670	319,599	2,009,043	0.16 : 1
USA, 1860	31,443,008	488,070	3,953,760	0.13 : 1

If you refer back to Tables II and III in the Eltis article that you downloaded, you will observe that the total number of slaves entering Barbados, Jamaica and St Domingue greatly exceeded their slave and free populations in the 1830s (or in St Domingue's case, 1791). The combined black and freed population of Barbados was less than 90,000, although nearly half a million slaves had been shipped to the island in the previous one and half centuries. Some of this discrepancy can be explained by intra-American shipments of slaves, but its principal cause was a chronic excess of deaths over births in slave populations in the tropics and semi-tropics. On the sugar plantations, death triumphed over life: the intense exploitation of labour, poor diet and the disease environment negated humankind's elementary compulsion to reproduce its own. The records of one Barbadian estate show that, between 1712 and 1748, 5 per cent of its labour force of 238 slaves had to be replaced each year (Watts, 1987, p. 366). Without continuous slave imports from Africa, sugar island populations would have decreased by a rate varying from 10 per thousand annually up to 40 per thousand annually (Curtin, 1969, p. 28). Fresh arrivals from Africa caused the vicious cycle of demographic wastage to persist because their mortality rate was higher than that of Creole slaves and their reproduction rate low, on account of unfavourable sex ratios. Only late in the history of Caribbean slavery was the point reached where the deficit between deaths and births diminished, the proportion of American-born slaves began to grow and fresh slave imports were only needed to open 'virgin land', such as Guyana. Barbados's population stabilised around 1810, but Jamaica's did not do so until the 1840s, after slavery had ended.

EXERCISE

What impact do you think the very high price of slaves at the beginning of the nineteenth century had on their treatment in the West Indies?

Spend just a few minutes on this exercise.

SPECIMEN ANSWER

They were an incentive for planters to improve the slaves' living conditions and to encourage them to breed.

DISCUSSION

There is evidence that rising prices had precisely that effect. Even before the abolition of the trade, planters began to clothe their slaves better, engaged doctors to care for the sick and women in childbirth, and instructed overseers not to over-tax pregnant slaves. To improve diets, more land was set aside for food crops. Abolition gave a further impetus to so-called amelioration as planters sought to establish a self-sustaining labour force. However, while mortality was reduced *fertility* remained low, and about half the female slaves in the British West Indies never bore a child. Several reasons have been adduced for this, including endemic venereal disease, which rendered many women sterile, and a protein deficient diet, which caused irregular ovulation. Furthermore, the planters' wish to see women slaves breed conflicted with the need to employ them in the cane fields, where they were in the majority in the labour gangs; the heavy work – normally fifteen hours a day but eighteen during the harvest – induced frequent miscarriages in the first stages of pregnancy. Added to which, post-natal mortality remained stubbornly high (Ward, 1998, pp. 429–32).

As I indicated on page 19, and Figure 13.8 makes clear, the historical demography of slavery in the thirteen colonies (and later the USA) was quite distinct, for there natural increase soon contributed much more to population growth than did the transatlantic trade. Around 1800, mortality rates for North

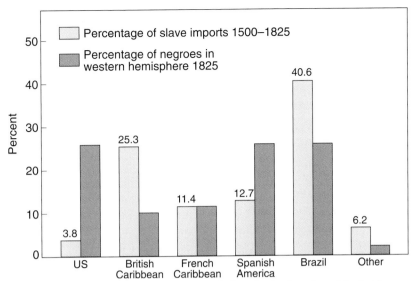

Figure 13.8   The distribution of slave populations in the Americas. Adapted from Fogel and Engerman (1974) p. 28, and Eltis *et al.* (1999)

American slaves were similar to Jamaican but their fertility was about 80 per cent higher. Had slaves in the United States duplicated the demographic experience of the British West Indies, the black population in 1800 would have been 186,000; in fact, there were 1.002 million blacks in the USA at that date. Although only 4 per cent of all slave imports were to the thirteen colonies or USA, well over a third of slaves in the western hemisphere lived in the USA in 1825 (Fogel and Engerman, 1974, p. 29).

quarter

Demographic decline in Africa?

As has been rightly said, demographically, the Americas were an extension of Africa, not Europe, until the early nineteenth century. So what was the demographic cost to sub-Saharan Africa of the export of 11 million slaves over three and a half centuries? Since there are no hard data for African demographic history before about 1900, one answer is that we cannot possibly know. But while we can have no knowledge from direct evidence, we can make certain deductions by extrapolating estimates of the early twentieth-century population and its historic rate of growth back into the past. This method is full of potential pitfalls, not least allowing for the severe 'Malthusian' crises which have periodically wracked Africa's population and render its historic rate of growth highly conjectural. Prolonged drought (always the principal cause of famine) and epidemics have been recurrent phenomena in African history. Their incidence makes counter-factual assessment of what the population would have been *without* the slave trade's demographic impact decidedly problematic. On one reckoning, slave exports merely skimmed off surplus people who would have perished anyway in times of social stress. But on another, the natural rate of growth was so low in Africa's harsh environment that even a proportionally small loss of fit young adults had large effects. Some scholars – whom I will call 'minimalists' – have inferred (partly from the preponderance of two males to every female exported) that the annual percentage loss in slave exports was well within the natural rate of increase and concluded that population growth would not have been much greater in the trade's absence. Others have argued that this ignores the lives lost in the wars and raids conducted with the specific purpose of gathering slaves, the deaths between capture inland and embarkation, and – crucially – the potential population growth had slave exports remained in Africa.

Patrick Manning has made the most rigorous attempt (so far) to measure the impact of exporting slaves over more than two centuries, using computer simulation to reveal changes over time in a demographic model (Manning, 1990). The great unknown in his calculation was obviously the population of sub-Saharan Africa around 1700: he estimated the size of that population by taking the 1931 population figures and applying a natural rate of growth, while factoring in the direct and indirect losses from slave exports. He was not exclusively concerned with the Atlantic slave trade: of the 14 million slaves exported from tropical Africa in the eighteenth and nineteenth centuries, about 5 million went to slave marts in the Islamic world. Nor, in estimating population loss, was he exclusively concerned with slave exports: people were killed in slave raids and mortality was high among captives; also, because captives were predominantly young adults, the fertility of populations raided for slaves fell. Manning postulated that 21 million persons were captured in Africa in the eighteenth and nineteenth centuries, 5 million of whom suffered death within a year of capture. What – Manning asked – would the population of Africa have been without the combined losses of the Atlantic and Muslim slave trades? If we assume a natural rate of growth of 0.5 per cent per year, the 'headline' figure is startlingly large: if the African population in c.1700 had been allowed to grow at this rate, 'the 1850 population of sub-Saharan Africa would have been roughly double that which actually lived in 1850: that is, it would have been nearly 100 million instead of roughly 50 million. Most of the difference was concentrated in the regions of the Western Coast, which suffered more heavily than the rest of the continent' (Manning, 1990, p. 85). If this were the case, the world's demographic balance was significantly altered: the African proportion of the combined population of the New World, Europe, the Middle East and Africa fell from about 30 per cent in 1600 to 10 per cent by 1900.

Compared with other counterfactual reckonings, Manning's erred on the side of caution, but his only reasonably firm datum was the total slave exports; the other figures were plausible guesses. Scholars have grave reservations about his assumption of a natural population growth rate of 0.5 per cent annually over several centuries. This is extremely low compared with population growth in contemporary Africa, but quite high by early modern standards. It implies the African population *could have* increased at the same rate as England's between the 1600s and 1850, which is doubtful given Africa's more hostile disease environment, periodic droughts and frequent famines. Yet, though a lower natural rate of increase would scupper Manning's counterfactual reckoning, it cannot support the minimalist claim that slave exports were well within the natural rate of increase. If African populations naturally grew very slowly, then it is more likely slave exports and the trade's indirect consequences induced stagnation or decline. For the moment the jury is out.

CONCLUSION

We have not done with the Atlantic slave trade; in a later unit you will study its abolition and suppression. But we have a reached point where we can summarise its role in the making of the modern Atlantic 'world'. Let us speculate as to what the New World would have looked like some three and a half centuries after the Columbian contact *without* the coerced immigration of 9.6 million African slaves. Since they accounted for three out of four migrants, the overall population would have been smaller. Crucially, the population and labour force in the tropical and sub-tropical plantation regions would have been a fraction of its actual size, and their output of export crops would have been negligible. Since only plantation crops and precious metals could bear the costs of ocean transport, the volume of transatlantic trade, which was the fastest growing sector of international commerce after 1720, would have been much reduced. The most prosperous region of the thirteen colonies (the south, where 40 per cent of the population were slaves in 1770) would have been less wealthy, and mainland British North America as a whole more autarkic and inward-looking. The Caribbean would have been a more peaceful place, since without black slaves the islands would have produced no sugar and would have been of trivial interest to the maritime powers. The indigenous population may have escaped annihilation, since the slave trade had the unintended consequence of bringing to the Americas nearly all the disease pathogens available in tropical Africa. This counter-factual speculation has the merit of bringing home to us the momentous impact of the slave trade on the shaping of the Atlantic 'world'.

REFERENCES

Austen, R.A. (1979) 'The trans-Saharan slave trade: a tentative census' in Gemery, H.A. and Hogendorn, J.S. (eds) *The Uncommon Market: Essays in the Economic History of the Atlantic Slave Trade*, New York, Academic Press.

Curtin, P.D. (1968) 'Epidemiology and the slave trade', *Political Science Quarterly*, vol. 83, pp. 190–216.

Curtin, P.D. (1969) *The Atlantic Slave Trade: A Census*, Madison, University of Wisconsin Press.

Curtin, P.D. (1990) *The Rise and Fall of the Plantation Complex: Essays in Atlantic History*, Cambridge, Cambridge University Press.

Eltis, D. (1991) 'Precolonial western Africa and the Atlantic economy', in Solow (1991b).

Eltis, D. (2000) *The Rise of African Slavery in the Americas*, Cambridge, Cambridge University Press.

Eltis, D. (2001) 'The volume and structure of the transatlantic slave trade: a reassessment', *William and Mary Quarterly*, 3rd series, vol. 58, no. 1, January, pp. 17–46.

Eltis, D., Behrendt, S.D., Richardson, D. and Klein, H.S. (1999) *The Transatlantic Slave Trade: A Database on CD-ROM*, Cambridge, Cambridge University Press.

Eltis, D. and Richardson, D. (2004) 'Prices of African slaves newly arrived in the Americas, 1670–1865: new evidence on long-run trends and regional differentials' in Eltis, D., Lewis, F.D. and Sokoloff, K.L. (eds) *Slavery and the Development of the Americas*, Cambridge, Cambridge University Press.

Fogel, R.W. and Engerman, S.L. (1974) *Time on the Cross: The Economics of American Negro Slavery*, Boston, Little, Brown, 1974.

Klein, H.S. (1990) 'Economic aspects of the eighteenth-century Atlantic slave trade' in Tracy, J.D. (ed.) *The Rise of Merchant Empires: Long-Distance Trade in the Early Modern World 1350–1750*, Cambridge, Cambridge University Press.

Manning, P. (1990) *Slavery and African Life: Occidental, Oriental and African Slave Trades*, Cambridge, Cambridge University Press.

Marshall, P.J. (ed.) (1998) *The Oxford History of the British Empire: The Eighteenth Century*, Oxford, Oxford University Press.

Price, J.M. (1991) 'Credit in the slave trade and plantation economies' in Solow (1991b).

Richardson, D. (1991) 'Prices of slaves in West and West-Central Africa: toward an annual series, 1698–1807', *Bulletin of Economic Research*, vol. 43, no. 1, pp. 21–56.

Richardson, D. (1998) 'The British Empire and the Atlantic slave trade, 1660–1807' in Marshall (1998).

Rodney, W. (1972) *How Europe Underdeveloped Africa*, London, Bogle-L'Ouverture.

Schwartz, S.B. (1987) *Sugar Plantations in the Formation of Brazilian Society: Bahia, 1550–1835*, Cambridge, Cambridge University Press.

Solow, B. (1991a) 'Slavery and colonization' in Solow (1991b).

Solow, B. (ed.) (1991b) *Slavery and the Rise of the Atlantic System*, Cambridge, Cambridge University Press.

Stein, R.L. (1979) *The French Slave Trade in the Eighteenth Century: An Old Regime Business*, Madison, University of Wisconsin Press.

Thornton, J. (1992) *Africa and Africans in the Making of the Atlantic World, 1400–1680*, Cambridge, Cambridge University Press.

Ward, J.R. (1998) 'The British West Indies in the age of abolition, 1748–1815' in Marshall (1998).

Watts, D. (1987) *The West Indies: Patterns of Development, Culture and Environmental Change since 1492*, Cambridge, Cambridge University Press.

UNIT 14

SLAVE PRODUCERS AND OLD WORLD CONSUMERS: COLONIAL TRADE, ECONOMIC GROWTH AND EVERYDAY CONSUMPTION IN BRITAIN, *c.*1700–1810

Bernard Waites

Learning outcomes

When you have finished this unit you should have the knowledge, understanding and skills needed to answer and debate the following questions and historical problems.

- What was the volume and composition of British international trade and, more particularly, *transatlantic colonial trade* between *c.*1700 and the early nineteenth century?

- How much of this colonial trade was *slave-based*?

- What were the profits of this trade and how were they consumed and invested in Britain?

- Did the direct profits of slavery accruing to plantation owners, together with the indirect, commercial profits accruing to merchants who dealt in slave-grown commodities, contribute significantly to the onset of modern economic growth in late eighteenth-century, early nineteenth-century Britain?

- At the core of modern economic growth was industrialisation, a process that profoundly transformed, first, select regions in north-west Europe and, later, economies and societies bordering the temperate North Atlantic. Was a necessary, though not sufficient condition for industrialisation the prior creation of transatlantic markets for British manufactures, markets that derived their own purchasing power from slave-based capitalism?

- What difference did burgeoning transatlantic trade in tropical groceries make to the everyday lives of British consumers?

INTRODUCTION – TIME FOR A CUPPA?

Some people look at the tea leaves to foretell the future; let us take a cup of sweetened tea and think about the past. The national brew never passed Shakespeare's lips. Tea and sugar were great rarities well into the seventeenth century; by the 1790s, they were commonplace. According to Frederick Eden, the pioneer social investigator, they were:

> now to be met with in most cottages in southern England ... Any person who will give himself the trouble of stepping into the cottages of Middlesex and Surrey at meal times will find that, in poor families, tea is not only the usual beverage in the morning and evening, but is generally drunk in large quantities even at dinner.
>
> (Eden, 1966 [1797], vol. 3, p. 533)

What had put these erstwhile luxuries on the tables of the poor? The short answer is the globalisation of trade and slavery. Tea was shipped from China in exchange for silver, itself mined in Spanish America, and for raw cotton and opium from India. Sugar was produced by African slaves in the British West Indies. To import these commodities on such a scale that they became mundane items of household consumption, Britain had to export its own goods and services to the wider world. Had it not done so, its balance of trade would have deteriorated. To put things simplistically, British producers had to become more productive to consume such imported 'luxuries' as sugar, tea and tobacco. So our cup of sweetened tea connects producers and consumers in four continents.

Now, savour the leaf's sharp tang, sense the sugar rush, and think of another course theme: state formation. The intercontinental commerce that put sweetened tea on the table was not driven solely by market forces and private organisations: it intermeshed with the mercantilist state. The East India Company had a legal monopoly on all British trade east of the Cape of Good Hope, the West Indian colonial sugar producers had a monopoly on the British market. Only British owned and crewed ships could legally trade with British settlements and plantations.

We can use our cup of sweetened tea to *allude* to the connections between slavery, colonial trade, economic growth and everyday consumption in Britain. But to understand them as historians we have to work a bit harder, using aggregate data to establish the big picture. Those unfamiliar with economic concepts – gross domestic product, investment, capital accumulation – have to acquire some grasp of them. The argument that follows may appear complex, but history is – in the fashionable jargon – 'a complexity science'. If this unit has an over-riding purpose, it is to strip our sweetened tea of its aura of simplicity.

Sugar Dynasty and the materials on the A200 website

DVD exercise

If you have not already done so, please view *Sugar Dynasty* on DVD 2 and read the accompanying notes in the *Media Notes*. The programme complements and reinforces what you learned in Unit 13 about the beliefs and prejudices that legitimated slavery and, without sensationalism, illustrates both the barbarity of the slave regime and the quasi-industrial process of sugar production. But I want you to use it here for another purpose: to get you to think about how the wealth generated by slave labour was 'consumed' (in the broadest sense of the word) in Britain and how slave-produced commodities affected the everyday lives of British consumers.

Spend about 75 minutes on this exercise.

In the section entitled 'Slavery, transatlantic trade and industrialisation', I will ask you to read extracts from secondary sources by Robin Blackburn and David Eltis, accessible through the A200 website, which bear directly on the question of how slave-generated wealth flowed into the British economy.

TRANSATLANTIC TRADE AND BRITISH ECONOMIC GROWTH

Unit 13 examined how the slave trade laid the foundations of the plantation economies which produced the principal commodities in early modern transatlantic trade: tobacco, coffee, rice, cocoa, indigo and, above all, sugar. Cane sugar was the single most valuable commodity import into Britain from the 1700s until the 1820s, when it was overtaken by another slave plantation crop – raw cotton. For much of this time, cane sugar was also the most valuable commodity import into France, which dominated the re-export trade in plantation produce for most of the eighteenth century. Whereas Unit 13 looked principally at Africa and the Americas, this unit has a British focus. We cannot entirely ignore French colonial trade because comparison with France is an invaluable check on arguments about the connections between New World slavery and British economic growth. If slave-based commercial capitalism was a springboard for industrial capitalism in Britain, then it should have played a similar role in France.

My purpose in this section is to establish the *value*, *geography* and *composition* of British foreign trade between *c.*1690–1815 and then to ask how important foreign trade was in the onset of modern economic growth.[5]

We are better informed about foreign trade than most aspects of the early modern British economy because of a relative abundance of quantitative data, derived from customs and excise returns. Taxes on imports have always been a convenient source of state revenue: they are inexpensive to raise and alienate fewer interest groups than land or income taxes because they tend to fall on luxuries, such as sugar. During the French wars (1793–1815) the escalating sugar duties were the most important single source of government revenue, accounting for one-eighth of all taxation.

Useful though foreign trade data are for economic historians, their interpretation is problematic, for several reasons. The taxation of trade is always an incentive to smuggling, and we can only guess at the dimensions of illegal trade. Sugar is bulky and requires sophisticated handling and storage

---

[5] Until 1707, Scottish trade was under a separate jurisdiction and even after the union Scottish trade statistics were collected separately. The data on the eighteenth century in the standard reference work (Mitchell and Deane, 1962) cover England and Wales up to 1772 (or 1791 in the case of specific items), Great Britain thereafter. Scotland accounted for about 9 per cent of British foreign trade in 1780. Trade with Ireland, a commercial and plantation colony of Britain, is separately itemised up to 1791. The British and Irish customs were not amalgamated until the 1820s.

facilities, so it is unlikely that substantial quantities were smuggled into Britain, but tobacco and tea were easily and profitably smuggled. In certain years, illegal imports probably accounted for a third of consumption. Imports and exports were recorded at 'official values', which diverged from market values as prices rose in the late eighteenth and early nineteenth centuries. The technical difficulties of converting 'official' to market values need not concern us, since scholars have concluded that the 'official' series are a fairly reliable indicator of changes in *volumes*. There is, however, a more intractable problem bedevilling the data on the re-export of 'colonial' produce, which formed a very substantial part of total foreign trade by 1800. When colonial commodities were re-exported, merchants were allowed three years to 'draw back' the duties paid when the goods entered Britain. This led both to delays in invoicing re-exports and their over-valuation, with the result that the quantities re-exported sometimes appeared to exceed imports. In the customs returns, retained imports of tobacco fluctuated so wildly in the later eighteenth century (from a trough of *minus* 9.2 million pounds weight in 1776 to a peak of 31.9 million pounds in 1788) that they are practically useless as a guide to domestic consumption.

EXERCISE

Tables 14.1–14.3 show the regional distribution of British domestic (i.e. home produced) exports and re-exports, and the regional sources of British imports during the eighteenth century. In case there is any confusion, trade *between* Scotland and England was internal trade and does not figure in these statistics, but trade between mainland Britain and the 'British Islands' (Ireland, the Channel Islands) was counted as foreign trade. Look carefully at the data and summarise the main trends. Bear in mind the outbreak of the American War of Independence (1775–83) and of the French revolutionary wars.

Spend about 30 minutes on this exercise.

Table 14.1 The destination of British domestic exports (£k, official values)

	Europe	British Islands (Ireland etc.)	Americas (inc. the West Indies)	Asia	Africa
1700–1 (England and Wales)	3,660 (82%)	144 (3%)	461 (10%)	114 (3%)	81 (2%)
1772–3 (England and Wales)	3,883 (40%)	912 (9%)	3,628 (37%)	824 (8%)	492 (5%)
1797–8 (Great Britain)	3,858 (21%)	1,641 (9%)	10,312 (56%)	1,640 (9%)	650 (4%)

(Source: Mitchell and Deane, 1962)

Table 14.2   The destination of British re-exports (£k, official values)

	Europe	British Islands (Ireland etc.)	Americas (inc. the West Indies)	Asia	Africa
1700–1 (England and Wales)	1,652 (77%)	159 (7%)	237 (11%)	11 (1%)	64 (3%)
1772–3 (England and Wales)	3,655 (63%)	1,102 (19%)	691 (12%)	69 (1%)	285 (5%)
1797–8 (Great Britain)	9,150 (78%)	1,286 (11%)	853 (7%)	75 (1%)	437 (4%)

(Source: Mitchell and Deane, 1962)

Table 14.3   The source of British imports (£k, official values)

	Europe	British Islands (Ireland etc.)	Americas (inc. the West Indies)	Asia	Africa
1700–1 (England and Wales)	3,578 (61%)	285 (4%)	1,157 (20%)	775 (13%)	34 (1%)
1772–3 (England and Wales)	4,301 (35%)	1,303 (10%)	4,522 (36%)	2,203 (18%)	80 (1%)
1797–8 (Great Britain)	7,003 (29%)	3,127 (13%)	7,678 (32%)	5,785 (24%)	62 (1%)

(Source: Mitchell and Deane, 1962)

With respect to exports, the most striking trends are the growth of markets in the Caribbean and continental America for British domestic exports and the stagnation of European markets. At the beginning of the eighteenth century, Europe absorbed four-fifths of domestic exports; at the end, one-fifth. Over the course of the eighteenth century, Ireland took a greater share of domestic exports, and provided a greater share of imports, and the Asian share of British trade also rose. It may be thought that warfare in the 1790s lay behind the relative decline of domestic exports to Europe, but then how do we explain the buoyancy of *re-exports* to Europe? The ships that carried coffee or sugar to European ports could surely have carried British woollens, cottons and hardware, had there been a demand. Table 14.3 underlines the partial decoupling of the British economy from Europe and its increasing dependence on other continents for imports.

These tables reveal the growing significance of transatlantic markets for British producers and shippers, and the British economy more broadly. Trade with the thirteen colonies collapsed during the American War of Independence, but this was clearly a temporary reversal since the 'Americanisation' of the domestic export trades accelerated with the restoration of peace. By 1800, nearly three-fifths of domestic exports went to the Americas. Independence freed Americans from the Navigation Laws and they now could import tea, coffee and sugar from wherever they chose, which explains the relative decline of re-exports going to the Americas

(Table 14.2). A point worth adding is that the 'Americanisation' of domestic exporting was all the more remarkable when we consider that Europe's population was about 200 million in 1800, while the combined population of the Americas was perhaps 15 million.[6]

Now let us consider the changing *commodity structure* of imports, domestic exports and re-exports as revealed by Table 14.4 (by commodity structure we mean the balance between manufactures, raw materials and foodstuffs). This provides three snapshots of the main goods shipped into and out of England and Wales in 1700 and 1760 and into and out of Britain in 1800. The table looks complicated and forbidding. So, rather than set a formal exercise, I have chosen to talk you through what we can deduce about the commodity structure of English/British trade at each snapshot and the major changes that occurred between them. Bear in mind that we are dealing with official values, not physical quantities: the two-and-a-half-fold increase in sugar import values between 1700 and 1760 does not mean physical imports increased two and a half times. Sugar was somewhat cheaper in 1760 and the quantity imported had risen more than three-fold.

The 1700 snapshot

In 1700, the commodity structure of English foreign trade reflected the country's commercial integration with Europe. Woollen goods accounted for nearly three-quarters of domestic exports by value. You should note that, apart from a small quantity of coal, nearly all domestic exports were *manufactures* or *semi-manufactures* of some description, a sign that England had a comparative advantage both in lush pastures (for breeding sheep) and handicraft skills. England was self-sufficient in food grains, but imported wine and raw materials for her textile trades and ship-building. The balance of trade was virtually neutral: imports were officially valued at £5.84 million, domestic exports at £3.73 million and re-exports at £2.08 million. This snapshot would have been broadly familiar to the early Tudors, but there was one novel element: the already substantial share of 'colonial' groceries (sugar, tobacco, coffee and tea) in the import schedule – together they accounted for over 17 per cent of imports. Sugar had been a rare luxury in Tudor times; in 1700, the value of sugar imports exceeded that of wine.

The 1760 snapshot

Several trends are evident. First, foreign trade values had grown very markedly. Total imports were now officially valued at £9.833 million (a 68 per cent increase on 1700), but the value of total domestic exports had risen much more rapidly. The total stood at £10.981 million, nearly a three-fold increase

---

[6] The population of the USA in 1800 was 5.3 million; the population of Latin America and the Caribbean may have been 10 million, though this is probably an overestimate.

Table 14.4   The commodity structure of British trade in 1700, 1760 and 1800

Principal imports, value (£)

	1700	1760	1800
Corn	–	–	2,673
Coffee	36	257	3,988
Sugar	668	1,799	4,301
Tea	14	969	1,510
Wine	647	371	732
Timber	119	147	582
Raw wool	220	91	500
Silk	377	626	739
Raw cotton	–	–	1,430
Tobacco	315	491	357
Iron	182	289	375
Flax	110	128	795
Hemp	71	58	507
Linen yarn	46	232	506
Other	3,035		
Total imports	5,840 (E&W)	9,833 (E&W)	30,571 (GB)

Principal domestic exports, value (£)

	1700	1760	1800
Coal	68	136	510
Iron and steel	90	539	1,605
Non-ferrous metals and manufactures	263	494	1,414
Cotton yarn and manufactures	24	167	5,851
Woollen yarn and manufactures	2,697	5,453	6,918
Linen yarn and manufactures	7	557	808
Silk yarn and manufactures	69	348	297
Other	513	3,287	
Total domestic exports	3,731 (E&W)	10,981 (E&W)	24,304 (GB)

Re-exports, value (£)

	1700	1760	1800
Coffee	2		11,068
Sugar	49	156	
Tea	2	256†	
Piece-goods	746†	1,353†	2,664
Tobacco	421†		624
Other			
Total re-exports	2,081 (E&W)	3,714 (E&W)	18,848 (GB)

E&W = England and Wales, GB = Great Britain

* = value of coffee, sugar and tea re-exports combined

on 1700. The balance of trade was highly favourable: combined exports and re-exports exceeded imports by £4.862 million. Second, woollens were still the most important item in the export schedule but their share of the total had fallen from 72 per cent to 49 per cent. Exports of linen, silk and cotton goods, and iron and steel had all increased at a much faster rate. Third, a large proportion of imports now arrived by oceanic rather than short-haul trade, and reflected British imperial and naval power. Imports of tea from China, the sole source at this time, had been negligible in 1700; by 1760, they had risen phenomenally. Imports of wine were much reduced. Sugar, tea, coffee and tobacco accounted for 36 per cent of all imports; if we were to include exotic fruits, rice, ginger, etc., then tropical or semi-tropical groceries made up two-fifths of imports. Except for tea, these were slave-grown crops.

The 1800 snapshot

This reveals an extraordinary resurgence of *re-exports*. They had increased five-fold since 1760, while imports had roughly tripled in value and domestic exports had roughly doubled. Re-exports handsomely corrected the unfavourable balance of domestic trade. You should note, too, that corn appears in the import schedule, indicating that Britain was no longer self-sufficient in food grains, along with substantial quantities of raw cotton. Raw cotton imports lay behind the thirty-five fold increase in cotton exports since 1780, and testify to the emergence of a dynamic, export-oriented industry in Lancashire. There is an anomaly in the data which you may have spotted: tobacco re-exports were, seemingly, nearly twice the value of tobacco imports: how are we to explain that? Had all pipe-smokers and snuff-takers suddenly quit the weed? Surely not; smuggling, delayed re-exporting and the over-valuation of re-exports may all have been involved.

Discussion

The 1800 data raise interesting questions about popular consumption that are germane to a later section. Coffee, sugar, tea and tobacco accounted for a third of all imports, but 62 per cent of re-exports. There is no particular virtue in selling goods to foreigners that could have been sold at home and it is difficult to believe that the home market was saturated. Living standards, we might conclude, were not rising fast enough to absorb the quantities available at the prevailing prices, which were inflated by high wartime duties. To which I must add there is a particular problem gauging the true scale of coffee imports and re-exports because the data are distorted by official over-valuation. Coffee imports *appear* to have risen ten-fold in the 1790s, but not because the British were seized by a craze for caffeine. Nearly all coffee was re-exported to European markets, which before 1791 had been supplied by St Domingue and other French islands.

The export data for cotton manufactures testify to the industry's role as the leading sector in early industrialisation, but beware of reading more change into the data than had actually occurred. Retained imports of raw sugar were worth considerably more than raw cotton imports in 1800, and sugar refining was a substantial 'industry', to use the word in its broadest sense. Imported sugar was not fit for the table, because planters in British colonies were prohibited from processing beyond the so-called muscovado stage.[7] All had to be refined before it could be distributed and sold, so substantial value was added in Britain. The industry was a useful foreign earner, since 'refined sugar' was classed with *domestic* exports, and accounted for 4.5 per cent of the total in 1800. Cotton yarn was mostly machine spun using water power, but cotton weaving was no more industrialised than sugar refining; in neither had machines and inanimate power been substituted for human effort and skill on any significant scale.

From the extraordinary total of re-exports in 1800, one could argue that the buoyancy of Britain's foreign trade sector depended as much on military might and shipping services as on the inherent strength of manufacturing. True, the schedule of domestic exports in 1800 was dominated by manufactures, as it had been in 1700, but *virtually all the increment was sold in relatively easy transatlantic markets*. Prior to the American war, the colonists had no choice but to depend on British suppliers for imports of manufactures, since the Trade and Navigation Acts effectively excluded all foreign goods. During the war, when Britain was confronted by the 'armed neutrality' of the major European powers, as well as the rebellious colonists and their French allies, exports slumped by about a third. With the resumption of peace, the Americans could import from whom they chose, and preferred British manufactures over all others. Does this demonstrate their quality and competitive price? Perhaps, but don't forget American import prices had to cover transport and insurance, sectors in which the British were very efficient. In 1806, when the Napoleonic system of economic boycott had closed many European markets for British goods, US customers bought about 35 per cent of British domestic exports and other American markets purchased a further 30 per cent. The closure of Europe to British goods had been partly compensated for by commercial access to the Spanish and Portuguese empires.

Export data are not very meaningful unless we can relate them to the totality of economic activity (gross national product – GNP) and the total output of manufacturing (gross industrial product – GIP) – see Table 14.5.

---

[7] My guess is that what the eighteenth century called 'muscovado sugar' was muckier stuff than the packet of brown sugar labelled 'muscovado' in my larder.

Table 14.5 Domestic exports as a proportion of gross national product (GNP) and industrial output + increase in exports as a proportion of increase in GNP

	(a) Domestic exports as a proportion of GNP	(b) Domestic exports as a proportion industrial output	(c) Increase in exports as a proportion of increase in GNP
1700	8.4%	24%	
1760	14.6%	35%	1700–60: 30.4%
1780	9.4%	22%	1760–80: 5.1%
1801	15.7%	34%	1780–1801: 21%

(Source: Crafts, 1985, p. 131)

Table 14.5 provides estimates of the ratio of exports to GNP and industrial output. We are dealing with an economy in the pre-statistical age so the speculative character of the data must be emphasised. Caveats aside, what do they tell us? Let's begin with columns (a) and (b). These show that the proportion of total domestic output exported in 1700 was 8–9 per cent of GNP, which was already quite high by historical standards. It would seem that around a quarter of manufactured output was sold abroad and so one in four non-agricultural workers already depended for their livelihood on foreign markets. The proportion increased significantly up to 1760, when the ratio of domestic exports to GNP of 14–15 per cent and just over a third of industrial output was being exported. This ratio was exceptionally high for a medium-sized pre-industrial economy. If you look at column (c), you will see that rising exports between 1700 and 1760 accounted for 30 per cent of the increase in gross national product (GNP). You will observe there was a severe check to exports' contribution to the growth of total output around 1780, caused principally by the American war. You should note that, though domestic exports recovered in the 1780s and 1790s, when the pace of industrialisation quickened, their contribution to the growth of total output was less than it had been in earlier decades.

EXERCISE

Using the information you have just acquired, answer the first question in the learning outcomes at the beginning of this unit: 'What was the volume and composition of British international trade and, more particularly, *transatlantic colonial trade* between *c.*1700 and the early nineteenth century?' In answering this question, what have you learned about the significance of slavery for British commerce?

Spend just a few minutes on this exercise.

SPECIMEN ANSWER

One-third of the commodity imports into late eighteenth-century Britain were produced by slaves and nearly three-fifths of domestic exports were going to transatlantic markets where slaves were an important, if not the principal, source of labour.

EXPORTS AND THE INDUSTRIAL REVOLUTION

You should now know more about the value, geography and commodity structure of foreign trade, and its ratio to total output, but what was its significance for the onset of the (first) Industrial Revolution, a process that initiated modern economic growth? The concept of the Industrial Revolution has two analytically distinct components: the first was *structural change* in the labour force, which resulted in a diminishing proportion of workers being employed in agriculture and growing proportions in manufacturing and services; the second was a generalised process of *technological innovation*, involving the substitution of inanimate power for human and animal effort, the mechanisation of handicrafts and the displacement of manual skills by machine operations (Landes, 1969, p. 1). The standard account of the Industrial Revolution portrays it as an *endogenous* process: that is to say, internally driven by population growth, improved productivity in agriculture and services, and rising incomes. Exports were, accordingly, a secondary factor. Advocates of the standard account do not dispute that an increasing proportion of manufacturing output was exported, but they do dispute the direction of causality: it was – they argue – the strength of the domestic economy that enabled British manufacturers to sell in export markets, not export markets that strengthened the domestic economy. In what is still the most thorough study of the long-run growth of the economy, Phyllis Deane and W. A. Cole pointed out that exports grew most rapidly when the terms of trade were worsening, in other words Britain was having to sell more abroad to fund its imports of tropical groceries and raw materials. When the terms of trade moved in Britain's favour, the rate of export growth declined. For Deane and Cole, the underlying dynamic in the expansion of international trade (imports and exports combined) was the *demand for imports* in a society where incomes were rising and consumer preferences were changing. They concluded 'if we want to understand the growing import demand [in eighteenth-century Britain] we must look for the factors which promoted economic expansion at home' (Deane and Cole, 1967, p. 89).

Why should we question this standard account? The reason is that the comparative study of industrialisation has revealed that structural change began at a very early stage in Britain, *long before* the mechanical inventions that revolutionised textile manufacturing in Lancashire. By about 1750, manufacturing, building, commerce and the professions already accounted for about 45 per cent of labour force allocation (Crafts, 1985, p. 13). Britain was unusual in undergoing such 'precocious' structural change; apart from the Netherlands, no other economy experienced such a pronounced shift of labour from agriculture to manufacturing at the proto-industrial phase of development.[8] Moreover, Britain was unique in the history of industrialising economies in having such a large proportion of manufactures in its domestic export schedule when the average income level was still very low. Those arguing that the Industrial Revolution was export led stress the role of foreign markets in raising the level of *aggregate demand* for manufacturing capital, labour and commercial services, and so boosting the growth of secondary and tertiary employment.[9] For an economy the size of Britain's, international trade was – so they maintain – a necessary condition for an extended market, a more complex division of labour and industrial specialisation. Ralph Davis was one of the first historians to make the connection between the dynamism of colonial exporting and the advance of manufacturing:

> The process of industrialisation in England from the second quarter of the eighteenth century was to an important extent a response to colonial demands for nails, axes, firearms, buckets, coaches, clocks, saddles, handkerchiefs, buttons, cordage, and a thousand other things ... In the iron and brass industries and all the metal-working crafts dependent on them, colonial demands made an important supplement to the growing home market, and must have played a considerable part in encouraging the new methods of organisation, the new forms of division of labour and improved techniques, through which the metal industries were to make a major contribution to industrial revolution in England.
>
> (Davis, 1962, p. 290)

This section has gone some way towards answering the fifth question in the learning outcomes at the beginning of this unit: *structural change* in the labour force – the movement of workers out of agriculture and into manufacturing and services – was to a significant extent induced by rising transatlantic demand for British manufactures.

SLAVERY, TRANSATLANTIC TRADE AND INDUSTRIALISATION

So what has this got to do with slavery and slave-based production? For a short answer, I can refer you to the intriguingly entitled *Africans and the Industrial Revolution in England*, by Joseph Inikori, a Nigerian scholar who has long been working on Atlantic history in the USA. Inikori's argument focuses on the vital contribution of Atlantic commerce to the expansion of

---

[8] Proto-industrialisation usually refers to a system of manufacturing in which merchants 'put out' the raw materials for artisans engaged on piece work in domestic workshops. Hand-loom weavers, chain and nail makers, glove and stocking knitters, and makers of the cheaper clocks were normally employed in this way.

[9] If you are unfamiliar with the terms, *primary* employment refers to work in agriculture, fishing and forestry; *secondary*, to manufacturing, processing, building and construction, and – usually – mining; *tertiary*, to work providing services (shopkeeping, schoolteaching, etc).

early modern international trade and the overwhelming importance of African slaves as producers of the commodities exported from the Americas. Free wage labour was scarce and expensive in continental America because the abundance of fertile land meant white indentured workers could easily become independent farmers after completing their labour contract. Large-scale commodity production was made possible only by importing African slaves, whose cheap labour enabled a growing number of European consumers to enjoy American commodity exports. The income from export sales in turn created American markets for British cloth, hardware, pottery and other manufactures, so raising the level of demand in the secondary and tertiary sectors of the British economy. The dynamic impact of Atlantic commerce on the British economy did not, Inikori argues, stem solely from Anglophone America. British-manufactured exports to Portugal and Spain were largely paid for by income generated in Iberian America, where African slaves produced sugar, coffee and cocoa, and were the mainstay of gold mining in Columbia and Minas Gerais.[10] Moreover, looking at the manufacturing sector of the economy as whole tends to disguise the crucial contribution of transatlantic sales to the expansion of production. If, as Inikori urges, we focus on the nascent industrial *regions* (Lancashire, the West Riding of Yorkshire, the west Midlands) we find their dependence on New World export markets was much greater than that of the long-established manufacturing centres of East Anglia and the south-west. The demand for labour in the buoyant export trades encouraged workers to marry younger and have larger families. Inikori concludes:

> The centrality of Atlantic commerce to the development process in England is the real measure of the contribution of Africans to the British Industrial Revolution. Apart from the forced labour of American Indians employed in the production of silver in Spanish America, enslaved Africans and their descendants were the only specialised producers of commodities in the Americas for Atlantic commerce.
>
> (Inikori, 2002, p. 481)

Inikori's argument is not entirely novel: when reviewing the role of exports in the growth of the British economy up to the 1770s, Patrick O'Brien and Stan Engerman underlined 'the significance of sea power, imperial connections, slavery, and mercantilist regulation for the sale of British manufactures overseas' (O'Brien and Engerman, 1991, p. 186). Where Inikori departs from other scholars is in asserting that without the export markets created by slavery and colonial commerce, industrial growth would have faltered and the British economy would have reached a plateau. Insufficient demand would have led manufacturing to stagnate, so there would have been less incentive to invest in

---

[10] Minas Gerais is a highland region about 480 kilometres (300 miles) north of Rio de Janeiro where gold was discovered in 1695; about 30,000 black slaves were mining gold around 1715.

technological innovation; capital would instead have flowed into commerce and financial services.

A critique of Inikori's thesis

Inikori has made an arresting case for making modern economic growth dependent on New World slavery. Is it intellectually persuasive? One criticism might be that it over-states the role of slavery in New World markets, which need disaggregating. These markets included Caribbean islands, where slaves were the great majority of the population, but also Pennsylvania and New England, which instituted gradual emancipation from 1780 onward and where political and social freedom were more entrenched than in Britain. The free, white population was increasing rapidly, and its purchasing power was several times greater than that of the slaves and slave owners: exports to the USA substantially exceeded exports to the British Caribbean from 1785 through to 1810. So can we assume that slavery's role in the growth of Atlantic trade was diminishing just as the tempo of British industrial growth was quickening? That would be a too hasty conclusion. The USA (particularly the northern states) ran a considerable deficit in Anglo-American trade. Transport costs restricted the British market for American produce to Virginia tobacco, Carolina rice and indigo, and, from the late 1790s, raw cotton, which were all slave-grown. So how did Pennsylvanians and New Englanders settle their accounts with their British suppliers? They could have shipped bullion across the Atlantic, but they mostly paid with credit notes, using earnings made by exporting food, rum and other supplies to the southern states, the Caribbean and Africa. In other words, slavery had a crucial role in the *multilateral* settlement of transatlantic trading accounts around 1800.

Had the United States remained within the territorial boundaries of the thirteen colonies, then we could envisage a steadily diminishing role for slavery in Atlantic trade, partly because the country was becoming more self-sufficient as the northern states developed their own manufactures. But the purchase of Louisiana in 1803[11] doubled the size of the nation and hugely expanded the area in which slaves would, in future decades, be the principal producers of export commodities. But that is a story we will take up in Unit 16.

Inikori's thesis can be more justly criticised, I think, for understating the complexity and resilience of the British economy and overstating its dependence on Atlantic markets. They absorbed between one-sixth and one-fifth of manufactured output in the last quarter of the eighteenth century: a sizeable proportion, to be sure, but insufficiently large to have the make-or-break developmental and demographic effects imputed to it. During the two conflicts with North America (1775–83, 1812–14) the British home market proved ample enough to prevent industrial collapse. But a more damaging

---

[11] 'Louisiana' refers to all the French territories on the North American mainland, which Napoleon sold to the USA in 1803.

criticism is that the thesis conflates those analytically distinct components of industrialisation to which I referred above.

Slavery was behind the growth of Atlantic trade and, because it extended the market, was a factor in 'precocious' structural change in Britain, but did it stimulate technological innovation? The links between slavery and British industrialisation *in this sense* were surely tenuous to the point of irrelevance. Its dynamics – common to much of Europe – were an exceptional technical creativity in harnessing natural forces for economically productive purposes and a competence in machine building unmatched by any other culture. There were, of course, manifest connections between cotton – the prototype machine industry – and slavery, but the causal relationship mostly worked from Britain *outwards*, with rising demand for raw cotton resulting in the extension of the slave plantation system. The mechanisation of cotton spinning is a classic instance of the shortage of an industrial input stimulating technical progress, for innovation began around 1770 in response to bottlenecks in the supply of yarn when the fledgling industry still obtained much of its raw material through the Levant. The productivity gains of mechanised spinning lowered the price of yarn dramatically, and led to increased demand both for cotton textiles and cotton fibre. Raw cotton imports rose eight-fold between 1780 and 1800, with Caribbean and Brazilian slave plantations meeting nearly all the rising demand. Obviously, there was a feedback from the New World as abundant supplies of cheap fibre became an incentive to further investment in cotton manufacturing in Britain. But mechanical innovation and the displacement of manual skills affected only the spinning and preparatory processes until the 1820s and 1830s, when power looms were introduced on a considerable scale. The cotton textiles that conquered overseas markets in the 1800s were woven by domestic handicraft workers using traditional techniques. By providing handloom weavers with cheap yarn, slavery enabled them to compete with the power loom for at least twenty years after the first viable model was patented. It *delayed* further industrialisation in the technological sense.

You should now understand the case for regarding slave-based transatlantic markets as a necessary, though not sufficient, condition for British industrialisation. You may have been entirely persuaded of its merits, but I think it needs modifying. With respect to structural change in the labour force, the case is fairly robust; with respect to *technological innovation* – surely an essential aspect of industrialisation – it is weaker.

THE PROFITS OF SLAVERY AND THE EMERGENCE OF INDUSTRIAL CAPITALISM

Up to this point, we have focused on slavery and the extension of the market. Now, we turn to slavery and *capital accumulation*. What do I mean by that? Well, we all know businesses must re-invest some of their profits to expand. The re-invested profits go into *capital goods* (let us say machines) which raise productivity and result in greater output. That, in a nutshell, is capital accumulation. What is true of businesses is equally true of national economies. To expand, they must raise their level of investment (accumulate capital) so that productivity rises and total national output grows. How poor agrarian economies, in which many lived close to subsistence, began the cycle of capital accumulation is one of the great conundrums of world economic history: they tended to become trapped at a low income level as population pressure forced people onto marginal land with a declining rate of return. Eighteenth-century Britain clearly broke out of this trap and entered a qualitatively new phase of economic growth; were the exceptional profits of slavery a significant contributory factor in that process? Several scholars have argued they were, most notably Eric Williams, the Trinidadian Marxist who later became his country's first prime minister. His *Capitalism and Slavery* (first published in 1944) remains a highly influential discussion of the historical relation between Caribbean slavery and the development of the British economy (Williams, 1961 [1944]). Its central contentions were that the slave trade and colonial slavery first paved the way for industrial capitalism by creating a stream of investment funds, and were abolished because they had ceased to be economically profitable.

Parts of the 'Williams thesis' are no longer tenable in the light of subsequent research into both the profitability of the slave plantation complex and the development of British economy. He greatly exaggerated the contribution of slave trading itself to capital accumulation in Britain: its profit level was under 10 per cent, and if we assume that the proportion invested was the same as the national ratio, then total investment derived from the slave trade was only £14,000 a year (or a derisory 0.11 per cent of total investment) (Anstey, 1975, Table 1, pp. 47, 51). As you will see in the next unit, the abolition of the trade was not economically determined, nor was the slave plantation complex in inexorable economic decline in the early nineteenth century. Furthermore, he overestimated the investment required for Britain's industrialisation because he, along with most economic historians of his generation, believed it swiftly transformed production techniques and business organisation. In fact, much manufacturing remained small-scale and was little affected by steam power in the 1840s. The investment requirements of the economy were, therefore, low: only 8 per cent of national income was devoted to investment in 1800, and 10.5 per cent in 1840. Countries industrialising later allocated much larger proportions of national income to investment. Williams imagined a surge of industrial investment, swollen by West Indian profits; in reality, investment barely kept pace with population growth between 1780 and 1820.

So what remains of value in the 'Williams thesis'? Some historians would say 'very little indeed'; others, that he correctly identified slavery's role in the emergence of modern, industrial capitalism. To explore those conflicting arguments you need to access the extracts from Blackburn and Eltis on the A200 website.

EXERCISE

Turn to the secondary source by Robin Blackburn, 'Primitive accumulation and British industrialization', on the A200 website. Blackburn's point of departure is Marx's concept of 'primitive accumulation' which, in volume 1 of *Capital*, helps explain the transformation of the feudal mode of production into the capitalist mode. In a capitalist economy, Marx argued, entrepreneurs profit by exploiting free wage labour; workers are paid less than the value they add in producing commodities. Entrepreneurs re-invest their profits in new or extended enterprises, thus accumulating capital. But the capitalist mode of production could not have originated this way, for there was no large class of free wage earners to exploit. There must have been some other way to kick start the cycle of investment, commodity production, profit and re-investment. Marx believed that the violent expansion of early modern Europe into the wider world provided such a stimulus: naked conquest and coercion led to the 'primitive accumulation' of resources in Europe; a process systematised in late seventeenth-century England when the state assumed new economic functions (such as managing the national debt and protecting domestic manufactures) while throwing its military power behind the colonial system (Marx, 1976 [1867], pp. 915–18).

Given that this is the guiding concept behind Blackburn's analysis, read what he has to say and answer these questions:

1   Does he defend the idea that industrialisation required a surge of investment? If not, why is investment a relevant issue? To what other types of investment does he draw our attention?

2   Does Blackburn claim that the profits of sugar production and distribution would themselves have greatly augmented the stream of investment funds? If not, what other profits does he regard as a source of 'primitive accumulation'?

3   Does he demonstrate that the direct and indirect profits of the 'triangular trade' supplied a substantial proportion of Britain's capital requirements?

4   What is the empirical evidence for industrial capitalism developing in close, causal connection with the 'triangular trade'?

5   Blackburn revises the 'Williams thesis' in a way that makes it more plausible; how is that?

Spend about 2 hours on this exercise.

SPECIMEN ANSWER

1   No; but investment remains a relevant issue because a commercial society trading much of its output abroad had to invest heavily in its transport infrastructure (canals, roads, harbours, docks) and urban improvements. Moreover, merchants and other entrepreneurs always needed working capital or commercial credit, which called for financial investment.

2   No; sugar profits could not in themselves have greatly augmented the stream of investment funds – though a substantial 'industry', sugar production and distribution were a small part of total production. However, substantial profits were *realised* by industries such as woollens, iron and, later, cotton textiles in New World and African markets, which would have been a fraction of their actual size without slavery.

3   No, he doesn't. He demonstrates that, on a conservative estimate, these profits *could have* supplied between a fifth and a third of Britain's capital requirements. Because they could have been used for productive investment does not mean they were. Perhaps West Indian fortunes commonly found their way into country

seats or extravaganzas such as Fonthill, which added little to the economy's productive capacity.

4 Empirical evidence has been found in the symbiosis between Liverpool merchants in the triangular trade and manufacturers in the nascent Lancashire textile industry. The merchants depended on local manufacturers (often proto-industrialists) for the supply of their most important trade goods, and so advanced credit. Manufacturers depended on export markets for long runs and economies of scale. Very little of the cotton industry's investment resources came from outside Lancashire; to a remarkable degree, it evolved within the Atlantic-facing mercantile complex based on Liverpool and Manchester.

5 Williams undermined his own case by arguing that the profitability of the plantation complex was in decline from the 1780s, whereas there is much evidence that its direct and indirect profits grew at least as fast as the economy as a whole.

DVD exercise

What impression did you derive of the profitability of sugar production from *Sugar Dynasty*? Bearing in mind Gad Heumann's critical comments on the programme's confused chronology, how would you explain one Beckford cousin dying a bankrupt while the other was celebrated as the richest man in England? How was Beckford of Fonthill's wealth invested?

Spend about 20 minutes on this exercise.

SPECIMEN ANSWER

The impression is a contradictory one. Sugar profits afforded Beckford of Fonthill a fabulous lifestyle, yet did not keep his cousin out of the debtor's gaol. We have no reason to think that Beckford of Somerley was an incompetent businessman and, since he directly managed his property, he was less prey to fraud than absentee planters. What the programme does not make clear is that he arrived in Jamaica when plantation profits were touching an all-time low, chiefly because of the American war and a series of devastating hurricanes. The estimated annual profit rate on an admittedly small sample of Jamaican plantations was only 3 per cent in 1776–82 – far below the rate of return on domestic trade and manufacturing. Beckford of Fonthill was from a wealthier branch of the family and his father had diversified into domestic commerce, finance and politics. This branch weathered the lean years of the 1780s and then garnered huge profits after sugar prices rose with the St Domingue revolution and the outbreak of war. Annual profits on Jamaican slave plantations were an estimated 13.9 per cent in 1792–1798 and 9.6 per cent in 1799 and 1819 (Ward, 1978). No domestic industry or trade earned this rate of profit over more than 25 years. Beckford invested his wealth in culture, architectural extravaganzas, conspicuous consumption and, briefly, politics. We do not know how typical this pattern of investment was, but the judgement made many years ago that West Indian wealth financed 'more Fonthills than factories' has not been seriously challenged.

Now turn to the secondary source by David Eltis, 'Europe and the Atlantic slave systems', on the A200 website. Eltis is possibly the sharpest critic of the 'Williams thesis'. The extract from his work is shorter than that from Blackburn; read it and answer these questions:

1   How, according to Eltis, should we think about the sugar islands in relation to the British economy?

2   What is his riposte to the argument that the triangular trade's direct and indirect profits could have generated a considerable proportion of investment funds?

3   There is a catch in arguing that, since the slave plantation complex generated such fabulous profits, they must have swelled the stream of investment funds; what is that catch?

4   Eltis insists we look at the relationship between the plantation complex and economic growth in a comparative perspective; how does this advance the argument?

Spend about 45 minutes on this exercise.

1   To gauge the real significance of the sugar islands for the British economy, we should think of them as specialised parts of the domestic economy that happened to be located thousands of miles of way. Their trade with the metropolis was more like trade between town and country than international trade; it is an accident of fiscal policy that we know so much about it. Viewed in this light, the sugar islands appear as small additions to a rapidly growing whole. The combined population of Barbados and Jamaica was about 300,000 in 1775, much smaller than that of Ulster, where the booming linen industry was located.

2   So could many other industries and their related trades. Although sugar was a big business around 1800, output and value added were several times greater in other industries, such as iron and woollens, which had stronger linkages to the rest of the economy. Their profits were absolutely, if not relatively, greater and rather more likely to flow into productive investment.

3   Those insisting on the stupendous profits made producing sugar must explain the incentive to shift savings to other sectors. If the rate of return was so attractive, why weren't sugar profits simply ploughed back into extending the sugar frontier?

4   The obsessive pursuit of causal links between New World slavery and British industrialisation looks bizarre in a *comparative* perspective. If any European economy should have been propelled into modern economic growth by the profits of slavery it was Portugal's: relative to its population – one-third the size of England's in the eighteenth century – Portugal's slave plantation sector was the largest of all the European powers. Portuguese and Brazilian capitalists must have invested a much larger proportion of national income in slaving and slave-based production than their British counterparts. Yet Portugal was steadily marginalised in the Atlantic 'world': it lacked internal transport systems, could not feed its own population, depended increasingly on imported manufactures, and was probably the poorest country in western Europe when the slave trade was finally suppressed. The French counter-example is equally pertinent: for much of the eighteenth century more slaves laboured in the French Caribbean, producing substantially more plantation produce, than in British America. In

1791, the slave population of the French empire was 50 per cent greater than that of the British and they produced considerably more plantation produce. France was a great manufacturing and commercial nation: the value of her transatlantic colonial trade rose six-fold between 1730 and 1776, a faster rate of increase than Britain's. By 1750, colonial commodities – sugar, coffee, indigo – represented more than half of French sales to the Dutch. Yet, though economic historians have traced the origins of modern French economic growth to the final decades of the *ancien régime,* none has argued the profits of slavery played a crucial role in the process.

So who is right, Blackburn or Eltis? We don't have the empirical evidence to confirm or refute their core hypotheses, but I think the argument is unlikely to be settled by further research, however desirable that is. Like all scholars trying to explain long-term development in modern world history, Blackburn and Eltis work within explanatory frameworks – or so-called paradigms – which have their own conceptual apparatus and which generate their own research problems. Eric Williams regarded New World slavery as a purely economic phenomenon which later gave rise to racism; Blackburn gives much more attention to the beliefs and ideologies that legitimated Atlantic slavery but regards its development as *primarily* determined by what Marxists call the 'forces and relations of production'. In other words, the dynamic underlying Atlantic slavery came from early modern capitalism's territorial expansion, which brought both the techniques of plantation production to the Americas and a highly competitive system of commodity production.

Eltis disagrees. In his view, European behaviour in the early modern Atlantic was not that of unbridled and profit-maximising capitalists: economic motivations were heavily circumscribed by a xenophobic culture from the inception of the plantation system. The problem he addresses is the *simultaneous* emergence of political and economic freedom and near absolute slavery within the jurisdiction of Europe's most liberal state; provocatively, he argues that we must look to Anglo-American freedom to explain Anglo-American slavery. (I touched on this paradox in the Block Introduction.) The same cluster of values and ideology that promoted liberty and free labour at home gave rise to absolute black servitude on the plantations. Englishmen in the colonies, who believed that private property was the bedrock of political freedom, and abominated slavery for their own kind, asserted absolute rights over legitimately acquired human property, provided it was black.

In so far as Eltis is concerned with explaining modern economic growth, his emphasis is on the endogenous sources of development in British society, its culture and values, as well as institutions and material resources. In this, he is part of an analytic tradition going back to Adam Smith, who never used the word 'industrialisation' and for whom a 'factory' was a trading station, not a site of productive industry. Smith identified economic growth with the division labour and the extension of the market, but his 'model' economy was primarily agricultural and commercial, with manufacturing capital (or 'stock') dispersed among myriad small producers. In the Smithian vision of history, economic modernity did not require a violent lurch to a new type of society; its origins lay much earlier than what we have come to call the 'Industrial Revolution'.

The Marxian vision is, as we have seen, quite different: the brutal dispossession of primary producers at home and the plundering of the wider world were preconditions for the emergence of modern industrial capitalism. Blackburn has endeavoured to substantiate this vision by demonstrating slavery's role in the advent of economic modernity in Europe. Eltis does not seek to diminish the significance of race-based slavery in the Americas, but in his view its strongest and most interesting influence on Europe was not economic, but rather ideological. I am not suggesting that either would dogmatically defend a position in the face of contrary evidence, but given their different frameworks of understanding, and the fragmentary nature of the historical record, it is not surprising they have reached such different conclusions.

So what, as students, should you seek to do? Try to understand the arguments and avoid stereotyping them as 'Marxist' (bad) and 'non-Marxist' (good). They should be accepted, modified or rejected in terms of their cogency and 'goodness of fit' with the evidence. My own view is that only a diluted version of the 'Williams thesis' is sustainable: Atlantic commerce *accelerated* the process whereby Britain emerged as a specialist mass producer of textiles, pig iron and a narrow range of machinery within a new international division of labour, but the fundamentals of this process were endogenous to the capitalist culture of north-west Europe (witness the speed with which the core innovations of the first Industrial Revolution diffused to the Belgian provinces of the Netherlands after 1815). But this is not a view I want to foist on you. If you find a stronger version of the 'Williams thesis' persuasive, argue for it. Above all, enjoy the intellectual frisson that comes with engaging with historical issues bearing on fundamental features of our modern, western world.

SLAVE-GROWN GROCERIES, POPULAR CONSUMPTION AND THE EMERGENCE OF 'CONSUMER SOCIETY'

You will have gathered that, from the 1700s, consumer demand for plantation staples was rising in Britain and in continental Europe's more prosperous cities. Clearly, more people were drinking sweetened tea, coffee and chocolate, using sugar to make their puddings and sweets, taking snuff and smoking pipe tobacco, but how quickly and how widely did these new consumption habits spread among the lower social strata? We tend to assume a linear progression from scarcity to abundance, from elite to mass consumption in the market for these consumer goods. But does the evidence bear this out? Let's consider first tobacco, which has long been the world's most popular recreational drug and could be considered emblematic of 'consumer society'.

Do the data for tobacco in Table 14.6 suggest a steady progression from tobacco's luxury consumption by a few to its commonplace consumption by the many?

Spend just a few minutes on this exercise.

Table 14.6   Annual per capita consumption of tea, sugar and tobacco in the UK (in lb, decadal averages)

	Tea	Sugar	Tobacco
1700s		See Table 14.7	2.3
1720s		See Table 14.7	2.3
1740s		See Table 14.7	1.65
1760s		See Table 14.7	1.5
1780s		See Table 14.7	1.0
1800s	1.42	19.12	1.11
1820s	1.24	17.83	0.79
1840s	1.54	19.45	0.91
1850s	2.24	30.3	1.1

(Sources: 1800s onwards – Mitchell and Deane, 1962, pp. 355–6; tobacco before 1800 – Goodman, 1993, p. 72)

Not at all. Assuming the data are accurate, per capita tobacco consumption peaked in the first quarter of the eighteenth century and then steadily declined over the next century. In the 1820s, consumption per head was about a third of what it had been in the 1720s. It seems most unlikely a lot of people were still smoking, but each smoker was smoking a lot less. As we know, tobacco is habit forming; you usually either smoke or you don't. To me, the data suggest tobacco was fashionable among men of all social strata in the early eighteenth century but – we might speculate – was generally confined to working men in the 1820s.

There are conflicting data on per capita sugar consumption in eighteenth-century Britain, but general agreement on how much was consumed in the decades after 1800 (see Table 14.7). Does the evidence indicate a linear progression from elite to mass consumption? What would a dip in consumption suggest about the general level of prosperity? How did consumption relate to wholesale price movements as shown in Tables 14.8 and 14.9? (If you convert pounds per year into ounces per week, you will get a better sense of how much was consumed in everyday life. For those unfamiliar with imperial weights and the pre-decimalised currency, there is a conversion table appended to this unit.)

Spend just a few minutes on this exercise.

Table 14.7   Alternative estimates of annual per capita sugar consumption in UK (in lb)

	Noel Deerr		David Richardson	Mitchell and Deane	
1700–70	4–8	1710	6.5		
		1731	15.7		
		1741	13.9		
		1751	15.0		
		1761	18		
1770–1800	11–13	1771	23.2		
1800–44	18 or less			1800s	19.12
1845–49	22.6			1820s	17.83
				1840s	19.45
				1850s	30.3

(Sources: Deerr, 1949–50, p. 532; Richardson, 1987, pp. 112–13; Mitchell and Deane, 1962, pp. 355–6)

SPECIMEN ANSWER

No, sugar consumption did not increase in a linear fashion either. On one estimate – though I believe an overestimate – annual consumption peaked at just over 23 lb per head in the early 1770s, and then fell back to around 19 lb. In the late 1790s, when the wholesale price of raw sugar touched a prohibitive 83s 4d per hundredweight (cwt) (as shown in Table 14.9), average consumption reached a plateau where it stayed until the 1840s, *despite falling prices after 1815*. There was a noticeable dip in average consumption in the 1820s when wholesale prices were tumbling.

DISCUSSION

How do we explain the fact that consumption dipped while prices fell? Well, sugar, unlike bread, was something a household could go without in hard times, so its consumption was a fair proxy for the general level of prosperity. For sugar consumption to drop while prices fell is a sure sign that household budgets were tightly stretched. As you might have deduced, real wages declined in the 1820s. Sugar consumption did not start to rise until the sharp reduction of sugar duties in 1846 and the harmonisation of duties on colonial and foreign muscovado.

Why do I think Richardson's consumption data are overestimates? His figures were arrived at by dividing retained sugar imports by the total population, and without making any allowance for the quantity 'lost' by refining in Britain. In reducing raw sugar to its more refined grades, between a quarter and a half was skimmed off in impurities. Assuming that most consumption was of the less-refined grades, I would suggest deflating Richardson's estimates by at least 20 per cent. If 20 lb of sugar per head were being consumed annually by the 1770s, that would have been just over 6 oz a week. This would have cost about 2d per head, with the average family of six spending a shilling a week on coarse sugar.

Table 14.8   Annual average sugar production of the British West Indies (tons) + wholesale price index (1700 = 100), based on current prices in the London market

	Annual average sugar production (ton)	Wholesale price index
1700–04	19,467	100
1705–09	17,729	78
1710–14	22,697	76
1715–19	31,691	77
1720–24	31,644	57
1725–29	42,875	56
1730–34	44,199	46
1735–39	41,170	51
1740–44	39,038	69
1745–49	39,383	84
1750–54	44,276	76
1755–59	55,247	90
1760–64	66,334	83
1765–69	70,436	85
1770–74	84,179	84
1775–79	72,998	109
1780–84	–	161
1785–89	–	–
1790–94	–	147
1795–99	–	193
1800–04	–	119
1805–09	151,897	90
1810–14	–	127
1815–19	156,037	113
1820–24	147,733	76
1825–29	136,546	71

(Source: Watts, 1987, pp. 288, 269)

Table 14.9   Annual price (shillings and pence per cwt) of muscovado sugar on the London market, 1665–1829, in five-year means

Years	Price	Years	Price	Years	Price
1665–9	50s 4d	1725–9	24s 3d	1785–9	N/a
1670–4	23s 6d	1730–4	20s 6d	1790–4	63s 4d
1675–9	21s 3d	1735–9	22s 0d	1795–9	83s 4d
1680–4	20s 3d	1740–4	29s 9d	1800–4	51s 4d
1685–9	21s 6d	1745–9	36s 6d	1805–9	39s 0d
1690–4	35s 3d	1750–4	33s 0d	1810–4	54s 9d
1695–9	39s 6d	1755–9	39s 0d	1815–9	48s 9d
1700–4	43s 3d	1760–4	36s 0d	1820–4	32s 9d
1705–9	33s 6d	1765–9	36s 9d	1825–9	30s 9d
1710–14	32s 9d	1770–4	36s 3d		
1715–19	33s 4d	1775–9	46s 9d		
1720–24	24s 6d	1780–4	69s 6d		

(Source: Watts, 1987, p. 269)

Sugar consumption, retail prices and household expenditure

The history of sugar (and indeed tobacco, though I will not discuss it here) is not just a matter of quantities consumed: the use, appearance and cultural meaning of the product changed greatly over the eighteenth and early nineteenth centuries. In the 1700s, and for some time thereafter, people spoke of *sugars* because there was no standardised commodity as we know it. Apart from its use as a luxury condiment, white sugar was widely prescribed as a medicine. One physician referred to 'nearly three hundred medicines made up with sugar' in a medical treatise of 1708. Another, Dr Frederick Slare, published *A Vindication of Sugars ... Dedicated to the Ladies* in 1715 which lauded the value of sugar as a dentifrice and as a cure for ailing eyes and the ailments of suckling babes (Mintz, 1985, p. 108). It was several decades before sugar acquired its banal significance as the universal, taken-for-granted sweetener.

Mercantilist restrictions forbad processing beyond the muscovado stage in the British Caribbean, so all colonial sugar was imported in a 'raw' state and had to be refined before it was fit for the table. Sugar refining was more akin to baking and confectionery than an industrialised process, and refiners produced different grades to suit different retail markets. Households could chose – according to taste and income – between 'single', 'double' and even 'treble' refined sugar, as well as between 'lump', 'loaf' and 'powdered' sugar. Wealthy customers usually bought sugar in the form of a 14 pound loaf, which would be attractively presented, like a bouquet. (*Sugar Dynasty* depicts luxury sugar consumption very nicely.) Retail prices reflected the different degrees of refinement: in 1744 and in 1771, the least refined 'ordinary' sugar retailed for 5d a pound, but a shilling a pound was being paid for a high-quality sugar loaf (Rogers, 1963 [1866–1902]). The Victorian scholar, Thorold Rogers, gathered fragmentary evidence on eighteenth-century retail prices for his monumental history of prices in England. This evidence indicates that the coarse grades were cheapest – and one would assume most widely available – in the early 1770s, which is consistent with Richardson's consumption data in Table 14.7. We can be sure that by then sugar had entered popular expectations of regularly affordable creature comforts. I must add that Thorold Rogers's price data, which were drawn directly from household account books, raise puzzling anomalies: for example, the retail prices of the *better* quality grades were stable in the late 1770s and early 1780s, despite the American war. Lump sugar could be bought at the same price in 1780 as in 1771, although the West Indian supply was drastically reduced and wholesale prices were rocketing. How can we explain this?

To us, the shilling a week the average household was spending on sugar in 1770 seems so trifling as to be meaningless; for eighteenth-century wage earners, it was a sizeable proportion of disposable income. Even a badly paid worker in contemporary Britain can earn the price of a pound of sugar in about 15 minutes; in the eighteenth century, it would have taken most workers half a day or more. Wages varied considerably between regions in 1700, though these variations had narrowed markedly by the century's end. In 1770, a London craftsman's daily wage in the building trades was just over 3s (36.67d) and a labourer's daily wage just over 2s (24.5d). Assuming a nine-hour day, the hourly wage was about 4d an hour for a skilled man, twopence ha'penny an hour for a labourer. Wages were about 30 per cent lower in the provinces. Money wages were quite rigid during the eighteenth century, though their purchasing power improved considerably with falling prices after 1725 and deteriorated with rising prices after 1770. In the south of England, real wages were generally lower in 1800 than they had been in 1700, though in the north they had risen by 50 or 60 per cent (Deane and Cole, 1967, pp. 18–21). Many workers – including those in urban trades – received payments in kind, so their real income when in work was more than their weekly wage, but only a fortunate minority were fully employed throughout the year. Essential food, rent and clothing probably accounted for two-thirds of all consumption expenditure in eighteenth-century Britain, with bread being by far the most important item in the average household budget. Bread was expensive in relation to workers' wages: a London labourer had to work more than two and half hours to buy a 4 lb loaf in the 1780s (see Table 14.10). A family of six needed two to three such loaves a day. Between half and three-quarters of a labourer's working time was spent earning the money to keep the family in bread. When bread prices rose steeply after 1800, the occasions when money could have been spared for sugar were few and far between.

Table 14.10   The price of bread in London (in pence (d) per 4 lb loaf)

1700s	5.25	1800s	11.96
1720s	5.26	1820s	9.94
1740s	4.76	1840s	8.6
1760s	5.74	1850s	9.46
1780s	6.43		

(Source: Mitchell and Deane, 1962, pp. 497–8)

EXERCISE

Go to the OU library catalogue, search for 'Eighteenth century collections online' as a title. When the catalogue entry appears, click on 'Eighteenth century collections online [electronic resource]' and in the next screen click on 'Linked Resources: Eighteenth century collections online'. When the 'Eighteenth century collections online' screen appears, search for 'Frederick Eden', the pioneer social investigator cited at the beginning of this unit. Several search results will be listed. Click on vol. 3 of *The State of the Poor* and then search for 'sugar'; you will come up with fourteen references. Go to the first on p. 710 and you will find the yearly household budget of an Epsom gardener's family. What is immediately evident about their expenditure on sugar and tea by comparison with other household expenses?

Spend about 20 minutes on this exercise.

SPECIMEN ANSWER

The family spent substantially more on tea and sugar than on rent, and more than it did on clothes, shoes or fuel. Sugar and tea, along with butter and cheese, were the third most important items of expenditure, after bread and meat. Sugar was 9d per pound – considerably more expensive than the coarse grades had been around 1770.

If you follow up 'sugar' in other household budgets in Eden's volumes, you will find that the pattern of household expenditure was generally much the same. Sweetened tea was pretty universally consumed by England's poor (though less widely drunk in Scotland and Wales) but it was also relatively expensive. Eden frequently alluded to rising prices and greater distress, and was evidently persuaded that working-class living standards were deteriorating. Whether he was right in this has been much debated by historians, but the evidence in Table 14.6 would clearly incline us to the view that daily circumstances of most consumers were becoming more straitened: per capita consumption of tea, sugar and tobacco *all* declined between 1800 and the 1820s. It was as if the eighteenth-century working classes had been beckoned to the emporium of consumer delights, and were then held at arm's length in the vestibule for two generations, with their modest doles of tea and sugar thinly stretched within the family until the prosperity of the 1850s.

Whether we can sensibly speak of the *mass consumption* of sugar in Britain before the mid nineteenth century is very debatable, for our judgement is bound to be affected by knowing what came later. Between 1870 and 1900, per capita consumption of sugar doubled in the UK (reaching over 90 lb per head per year at the turn of the century) principally because of the onset of mass-produced biscuits, cakes, chocolate, soft drinks and other sweetened foodstuffs. In 1900, the wholesale price of sugar was 11s 3d per cwt, which as you can see from Table 14.9 was far below eighteenth- and early nineteenth-century prices, when the purchasing power of money was greater. Even when rationed during the two world wars, the passive consumption of sugar in processed food and drink meant that considerably more was consumed per head in Britain than at *any time* before 1865.

I emphasise this to put changes in eighteenth- and early nineteenth-century consumption habits within a long-term perspective. Some historians – including Blackburn – have made large claims for sugar as a supplement to the otherwise deteriorating diet of working people during early industrialisation and as a palliative for their poorer quality of life generally. These assertions seem somewhat implausible in view of the likely quantities being consumed in workers' households.

Whose 'consumer society'?

Many people in mid eighteenth-century England took consumer luxuries for granted and were coming to live in what we would now call 'consumer society'. Proportionately fewer did in Scotland and Wales because living standards were lower. Britain, though more particularly England, was the wealthiest and most rapidly urbanising society of its day, accounting for nearly three-quarters of urban European population growth between 1750 and 1800. The landed aristocracy was unquestionably the nation's ruling class (and scarcely more permeable to outsiders than the Continental nobility), but in the cities and larger towns, merchants, shopkeepers, lawyers, apothecaries, master craftsmen, brewers, confectioners and a host of other tradesmen constituted a large, socially open 'middling sort'. The middle ranks of society, with family incomes between £50 and £200 a year, comprised nearly 25 per cent of the population by the 1780s. There were, of course, staggering disparities of wealth, but between the extremes of riches and poverty had emerged a large class of moderately prosperous property holders able to enjoy what Adam Smith called the 'decencies' of life, including exotic foodstuffs, snuff and imported cottons. They were the social backbone of 'a polite and commercial people' for whom shopping and shopkeeping had become vital socio-economic activities. Tax officials recorded 141,700 retail outlets in England and Wales in 1759, of which 21,603 were in London. Urban space was reconfigured to accommodate shoppers. Fashionable shops clustered in brightly lit, well-paved shopping streets, such as the Strand, where shopkeepers developed the art of window display, while advertising their wares and services in handbills and trade directories (Brewer, 1997, p. xxvii). The market for slave-grown groceries in Britain was symptomatic of the way the respectable habits of an emerging consumer society permeated a wide social stratum. Offering sweetened tea, snuff and pipe tobacco became rituals of polite hospitality and entwined with cultural norms of domesticity and sociability. They helped mark out domestic space, since men were often expected to smoke separately from women.

CONCLUSION AND REPRISE

This unit has been principally concerned with economic development and socio-cultural change in Britain, which by eighteenth-century standards was an egregiously free society. Unlike a vast swathe of central and eastern Europe, it had no class of coerced producers and no caste-like groups who were poor simply because of their hereditary status. The possibility of enjoying a considerable margin over bare subsistence was open to all and much consumption was of non-essential goods that gave pleasure and/or prestige. It seems stating the obvious to say that consumption was determined by the purchasing power of individuals and households, but we should not take this characteristic of modernity for granted. The medieval church had attempted to regulate consumption for theological and moral reasons. In *ancien régime* monarchies, the nobility was a closed social order with consumption rights setting it apart from the peasantry and the bourgeoisie. Britain (like the Netherlands) had become a society in which consumption largely determined status.

Viewed in a long-term and comparative perspective, eighteenth-century Britain also stands out as a society in which production and consumption had become sharply differentiated functions, and where daily activity was clearly divided between economically productive work and household consumption. This had not always been so. In the old manorial economy – which persisted over much of Europe into the early nineteenth century – the great rural majority were both producers and consumers: they produced their own subsistence, that is food, and may well have produced some essential consumer goods, such as cloth and wooden clogs, within the household. By the eighteenth century, such self-sufficiency was rarely found in Britain: nearly all production was for exchange; there was a clear division of labour between town and country, and between agriculture and urban manufacturing and services. The market for consumer goods (food and non-food) was already well organised; distribution and retailing were becoming specialised services. Shopkeepers in the larger towns and cities were as much in the vanguard of economic modernity as manufacturers: witness the many ploys adopted to attract and retain custom – glossy packaging, advertising, offering credit, selling 'loss leaders'.

For a long time, the emergence of modern consumer society in Britain was overshadowed as a subject for scholarly investigation by the Industrial Revolution, a process which brought a step change in the rate of economic growth, first in Britain, then in north-west Europe and New England. I remain persuaded that industrialisation opened a great divide in human society and understanding the process ought to be part of every historical education. Nevertheless, a preoccupation with industrialisation has occluded the pace and scale of socio-economic change *before* technological innovation in textiles revolutionised mass manufacturing.

Much of that change was integrally related to the construction of a 'maritime-imperial system', based on naval power, merchant shipping and long-distance trade. The colonial trades were the 'rich trades', which earned large profits but required considerable capital and advanced skills in banking, insurance and the management of shipping. As our leading naval historian puts it:

> To a greater and greater extent, Britain's real wealth was generated, and seen to be generated, from a maritime system in which overseas trade created the income which paid for the Navy, merchant shipping trained the seamen which manned it, so that the Navy in turn could protect trade and the country.
>
> (Rodger, 2004, p. 180)

The most dynamic of the 'rich trades' were with the slave plantation complex, which provided British consumers with their favourite luxury goods, sugar and tobacco, and increasingly with a major industrial input – raw cotton. And we should add that the income stream from re-exporting plantation produce was vital to financing the French wars, which became a global struggle to defend and extend the 'maritime-imperial system'. So both everyday consumption in Britain, which was becoming a free-market society, and the military-fiscal power of the British imperial state, were intimately connected with slavery and slave-driven commerce.

The stark obverse of bustling consumerism and socio-economic freedom at home was black slavery in the plantation colonies. Free-market capitalism and slave-based capitalism had common ideological and institutional roots in the rights of private property. In the context of the early modern Atlantic commerce, they were mutually supportive economic systems. Without slavery, the volume of Atlantic commerce would have been much smaller, and without Atlantic commerce, the extent of the market would have been much reduced. Only late in the eighteenth century, for reasons we will explore in the next unit, did the essential nexus between these systems – the Atlantic slave trade – come to seem morally intolerable, and it was another three decades before slavery was abolished in Britain's colonies.

REFERENCES

Anstey, R. (1975) *The Atlantic Slave Trade and British Abolition*, Basingstoke, Macmillan.

Brewer, J. (1997) *The Pleasures of the Imagination: English Culture in the Eighteenth Century*, London, HarperCollins.

Crafts, N.C.R. (1985) *British Economic Growth During the Industrial Revolution*, Oxford, Oxford University Press.

Davis, R. (1962) 'English foreign trade, 1700–1774', *Economic History Review*, 2nd series, vol. 15, no. 2, pp. 285–303.

Deane, P. and Cole, W.A. (1967) *British Economic Growth 1688–1959*, 2nd edn, Cambridge, Cambridge University Press.

Deerr, N. (1949–50) *A History of Sugar*, 2 vols, London, Chapman and Hall.

Eden, F. (1966 [1797]) *The State of the Poor*, 3 vols, facsimile edition, London, Frank Cass.

Goodman, J. (1993) *Tobacco in History: The Cultures of Dependence*, London, Routledge.

Inikori, J.E. (2002) *Africans and the Industrial Revolution in England: A Study in International Trade and Economic Development*, Cambridge, Cambridge University Press.

Landes, D.S. (1969) *The Unbound Prometheus: Technological Change and Economic Development in Western Europe since 1750*, Cambridge, Cambridge University Press.

Marx, K. (1976 [1867]) *Capital*, vol.1, Harmondsworth, Penguin.

Mintz, S.W. (1985) *Sweetness and Power: The Place of Sugar in Modern History*, Viking, New York.

Mitchell, B.R. and Deane, P. (1962) *Abstract of British Historical Statistics*, Cambridge, Cambridge University Press.

O'Brien, P.K. and Engerman, S.L. (1991) 'Exports and the growth of the British economy from the Glorious Revolution to the Peace of Amiens', in Solow, B.L. (ed.) *Slavery and the Rise of the Atlantic System*, Cambridge, Cambridge University Press.

Richardson, D. (1987) 'The slave trade, sugar and British economic growth, 1748–1776' in Solow, B.L. and Engerman, S.L. (eds) *British Capitalism and Caribbean Slavery*, Cambridge, Cambridge University Press.

Rodger, N.A.M. (2004) *The Command of the Ocean: A Naval History of Britain, 1648–1815*, London, Allen Lane.

Rogers, J.E.T. (1963 [1866–1902]) *A History of Agriculture and Prices in England*, vol. 7, *1703–1793*, Vaduz, Kraus Reprint.

Schumpeter, E.B. (1960) *English Overseas Trade Statistics 1697–1808*, Oxford, Clarendon Press.

Ward, J.R. (1978) 'The profitability of sugar planting in the British West Indies, 1650–1834', *Economic History Review*, new series, vol. 31, no. 2, May, pp. 197–213.

Watts, D. (1987) *The West Indies: Patterns of Development, Culture and Environmental Change since 1492*, Cambridge, Cambridge University Press.

Williams, E. (1961 [1944]) *Capitalism and Slavery*, Chapel Hill, University of North Carolina Press reprint.

APPENDIX

Britain did not adopt a decimalised currency system until 1967. Before then, £1 was equal to 20 shillings (usually written as 20/- or 20s) and there were 12 pennies (written as 12d) in every shilling. Under the imperial system of weights and measures commonly in use up to the 1970s:

16 ounces = 1 lb (453.5 grams)
14 lb = 1 stone (6.097 kilograms)
112 lb = 1 hundredweight (50.792 kilograms)
2,240 lb = 1 ton (or long ton) (1.01584 metric tons)

Bernard Waites

Learning outcomes

When you have finished this unit you should have the knowledge,
understanding and skills needed to answer and debate the following questions
and historical problems.

- Why did the Haitian slave rebellion succeed when all other slave
  uprisings in modern times have failed?

- What was the role of the French Revolution in ensuring this success?

- How and why was the British parliament persuaded to enact the
  abolition of the slave trade?

- Why was there a hiatus of some two decades between abolition of the
  slave trade in 1807 and the launching of a mass movement in favour of
  slave emancipation in Britain's colonies?

- What role did slave resistance and rebellion play in persuading the
  British political class that colonial slavery had to be terminated?

INTRODUCTION

DVD exercise

Before embarking on this unit, I would like you to view the second slavery
programme on the DVD 2, *Breaking the Chains*, which will form the basis of
your work on the third section. Please make notes on these points:

- the attitude of William Wilberforce to colonial slavery after parliament abolished
  the slave trade in 1807

- the impact of measures to regulate and reform colonial slavery on slaves
  themselves

- the role of white evangelical missionaries in slave communities in the 1820s and
  1830s

- the onset of a widely supported campaign to end colonial slavery in Britain after
  1823 (What was its main moral source? How did it mobilise public opinion?)

- the part played by slave resistance in ending colonial slavery.

Spend about 90 minutes on this exercise.

From the 1780s, the Atlantic slave trade and colonial slavery in the Americas came under sustained moral, political and revolutionary assault. This unit focuses on three key dramas in that assault. The first was the destruction of slavery in Europe's most valuable colony, St Domingue, which began with the slave rebellion in August 1791 and ended with the proclamation of the Republic of Haiti on 1 January 1804. The second was the long campaign to abolish the Atlantic slave trade, which culminated in the outlawing of the trade by the British and US legislatures in March 1807. The third was the enactment of slave emancipation in Britain's colonial empire, which came into force in January 1834.

Is that straightforward? Then let me keep things complex. It would have been no less true to have written: 'from the 1800s, most American regions depending on slaves to produce their export commodities entered a golden age'. The 1807 Act did not end the slave trade, though enforcement of the Act after 1815 did make it more hazardous and costly, and emancipation did not follow automatically from abolition. With or without an external supply of slaves, slavery was an expanding system of production in the Americas during

Figure 15.1   The West Indies, *c.*1789, from James Walvin, *Atlas of Slavery*, Harlow, Pearson Education Ltd, 2006, map 48

the first half of the nineteenth century. From the 1820s, the new technologies of the Industrial Revolution enabled capitalists to extend the slave plantation system in Spanish Cuba and Puerto Rico, the US south and in south-east Brazil. Only with hindsight can the events we shall be considering be interpreted as part of a linear and global movement 'from slavery to freedom'.

The unit is linked with all the overarching themes of A200: it examines the beliefs and ideologies that animated the abolitionist movement, the black revolutionaries and the campaign to emancipate the slaves. It considers more briefly how abolition and emancipation impacted on the production of plantation commodities in the British Caribbean and their consumption in Britain. It is concerned with the formation of the state of Haiti, but more importantly – in terms of its impact on the wider world – with the re-formation of the links between civil society and political power in Britain. The emancipation of colonial slaves would not have occurred without the larger movement of political reform, which resulted in the 1832 Reform Act. Henceforth, an anti-slavery stance was integral to the remaking of Britain as an aggressively liberal state seeking a 'new world order' in which free trade and free labour could flourish; without belittling the moral force behind this stance, it is essential to observe how it served national interests.

THE ENLIGHTENMENT, EVANGELICAL CHRISTIANITY AND ANTI-SLAVERY SENTIMENT

In February 1794, the National Convention of the new French Republic voted to abolish slavery in all French territories, without compensating the slave owners. Its brief decree declared that 'all men, without distinction of colour, domiciled in the colonies, are French citizens and enjoy all the rights assured under the Constitution' (quoted in Blackburn, 1988, p. 225). The puzzling thing is not why the French revolutionaries took this step but why it took them so long to honour their libertarian principles. The intellectual battle against the institution of slavery had been won long before the estates general were summoned in 1788, if we are to judge from the writings of Europe's leading secular thinkers. In mid eighteenth-century France, the progressive secular thought of the radical Enlightenment was distilled in the multi-volume *Encyclopédie*, edited by Dennis Diderot and d'Alembert – a stupendous collective effort to demonstrate that human affairs could and should be subject to reason and science, rather than faith and dogma. The articles on 'Esclavage' (slavery) and 'Traite des nègres' (the slave trade) were not original pieces; their author, Louis de Jaucourt, was a minor Enlightenment figure who drew heavily on Montesquieu for the first and plagiarised a contemporary Scottish jurist for the second. But publication in the *Encyclopédie* gave them a particular authority and wide currency.

EXERCISE

Turn to the extracts from these articles that are supplied as Anthology Document 4.4, 'Enlightenment definitions of slavery', and summarise their main points.

Spend about 20 minutes on this exercise.

SPECIMEN ANSWER

In nature, men were born free; slavery was contrary to natural and civil law. The slave trade violated religion, morality, natural laws and 'all the rights of human nature'.

Enlightened opinion in Britain was equally hostile to slavery. The Scottish political economists – pre-eminently Adam Smith – put free labour at the moral core of their scientific enquiry into what we now call modern economic development. 'The property which every man has in his own labour', wrote Smith in 1776, 'as it is the original foundation of all other property, so it is the most sacred and inviolable' (Smith, 1910 [1776], p. 110). Smith took this idea from John Locke, whose influence was briefly discussed in the Block Introduction, but was more consistent in condemning slavery in all circumstances. Smith believed it was economically irrational, as well as immoral, to exact another person's labour by force.

EXERCISE

Turn to Anthology Document 4.5, 'Adam Smith, *An Inquiry into the Nature and Causes of the Wealth of Nations*' and make a note of Smith's argument.

Spend about 10 minutes on this exercise.

By the 1820s, Smith's argument had become part of the 'common sense' of the British political class. In 1831, a member of the cabinet, Lord Goderich, used it when instructing officials to emancipate all slaves owned by the crown.

In the Anglophone world, intellectual arguments against slavery resonated with a widening community of anti-slavery sentiment whose principal source was evangelical Protestantism. As a religious mindset, evangelicalism is not easy to define: in the later eighteenth century, an evangelical was usually someone who had been overwhelmed by a crushing sense of personal sin and come to realise that salvation lay only in faith in the redeeming power of Christ's sacrifice. Evangelicals were energised by a moral fervour which set them apart from other Christians: they undertook good works because 'charity' – meaning selfless love of others – was Christ's injunction and because they thereby demonstrated their faith. Evangelicalism was a transatlantic phenomenon, associated both with the moral reform of the established church and the emergence of new dissenting sects (principally the Methodists, who became a separate denomination after John Wesley's death in 1791).

By 1780, although commentaries were still being published on the Biblical sanctions for slavery, the balance of Protestant theology had shifted towards condemning the institution as contrary to God's will. An anti-slavery ethic had slowly evolved among the American Quakers before being transmitted back across the Atlantic. The incompatibility of slavery and slave trading with

Christian principles was first urged at the yearly meeting of the Pennsylvania Society of Friends in 1688. In 1774, the Pennsylvania and New Jersey Quakers finally resolved to exclude slave traders and slave owners from their society. Quakers formed the large majority of the committee that met in London to set up 'A Society for Effecting the Abolition of the Slave Trade' in April 1787. This was a key moment in turning anti-slavery sentiment into political action, for the society brought together dissenting tradesmen with a few upper-class evangelical Anglicans. Pre-eminent among them was Thomas Clarkson (see Figure 15.2), who gave up a glittering career in the established church to be the society's principal investigator and publicist – roles he performed with great energy and skill, becoming the indispensable pivot between anti-slavery sentiment in the country and the parliamentary elite.

Figure 15.2   Carl Frederik von Breda, *Thomas Clarkson*, 1788, oil on canvas, 90.8 x 70.5 cm. National Portrait Gallery, London. Photo: © National Portrait Gallery

Thomas Clarkson (1760–1846) was born in Wisbech and educated at the grammar school where his father, an Anglican priest, was headmaster. In 1785, he won a Cambridge University prize for an essay on the question: 'Is it lawful to enslave the unconsenting?' This was published, by a Quaker bookseller, as *An Essay on the Slavery and Commerce of the Human Species, Particularly the African*, in 1786. In the early summer of 1787, Clarkson began the exhaustive – and exhausting – investigations on behalf of the Committee for the Abolition of the Slave Trade which took him to every slaving port. In 1789–90, he spent five months in Paris trying to persuade the National Assembly to abolish the slave trade. As well as having a crucial role in securing the 1807 Act abolishing the trade, Clarkson was instrumental in ensuring its enforcement. He attended the Paris peace conference in 1814 and the 'summit meeting' of the major states at Aix-la-Chapelle in 1818 as an unofficial ambassador for anti-slavery. With the formation of the Anti-slavery Society in 1823, Clarkson threw himself into the campaign for gradual emancipation. In the 1830s, he lent his prestige and pen to the American abolition movement, and presided over the international anti-slavery convention held in London in June 1840.

The most important 'voice' we must attend to in the struggle to deny slavery moral legitimacy is that of the slaves and former slaves themselves. Slaves had always resisted their slavery and, in inaccessible areas of the larger colonies, escaped slaves and their descendants formed 'maroon' communities. Some became more or less permanent micro-polities, grudgingly acknowledged by colonial governors. Black scholars have seen *marronage* (to use the French term) as part of a continuum of slave resistance running from petty sabotage – when slaves surreptitiously broke tools or damaged crops – to mass rebellion. This is a problematic interpretation: maroons certainly represented escape, defiance and autonomy, but they rarely questioned the legitimacy of slavery as such. Planters not infrequently used them to hunt down absconding slaves. This should not surprise us, any more than the fact that former slaves occasionally became slave owners. To comprehend slavery as an unjust and immoral institution needed a framework of understanding in which freedom was seen either as divinely willed or a universal human right. Such a framework could only come with literacy and what we call 'discursive reasoning'. By the 1780s, emancipated and educated slaves were engaging with the Bible, where they found a powerful myth of redemption from slavery in the Book of Exodus, but also with the secular rationalism of the Enlightenment. Two former slaves, Olaudah Equiano and Ottobah Cugoano, wrote autobiographical narratives in the 1780s and both became celebrated witnesses against the slave trade at abolitionist meetings (see Figures 15.3 and 15.4).[12]

---

[12] Slave narratives are extensively discussed in Block 4 of the Open University course A207 *From the Enlightenment to Romanticism*, which is why this fascinating topic is only touched on here. There is conclusive documentary evidence that Equiano was born on a Carolina slave plantation and was not, as he claimed, an African of noble birth who had been kidnapped in the interior. Cugoana's account of his Fante childhood, enslavement and sale to white traders on the coast seems to be authentic.

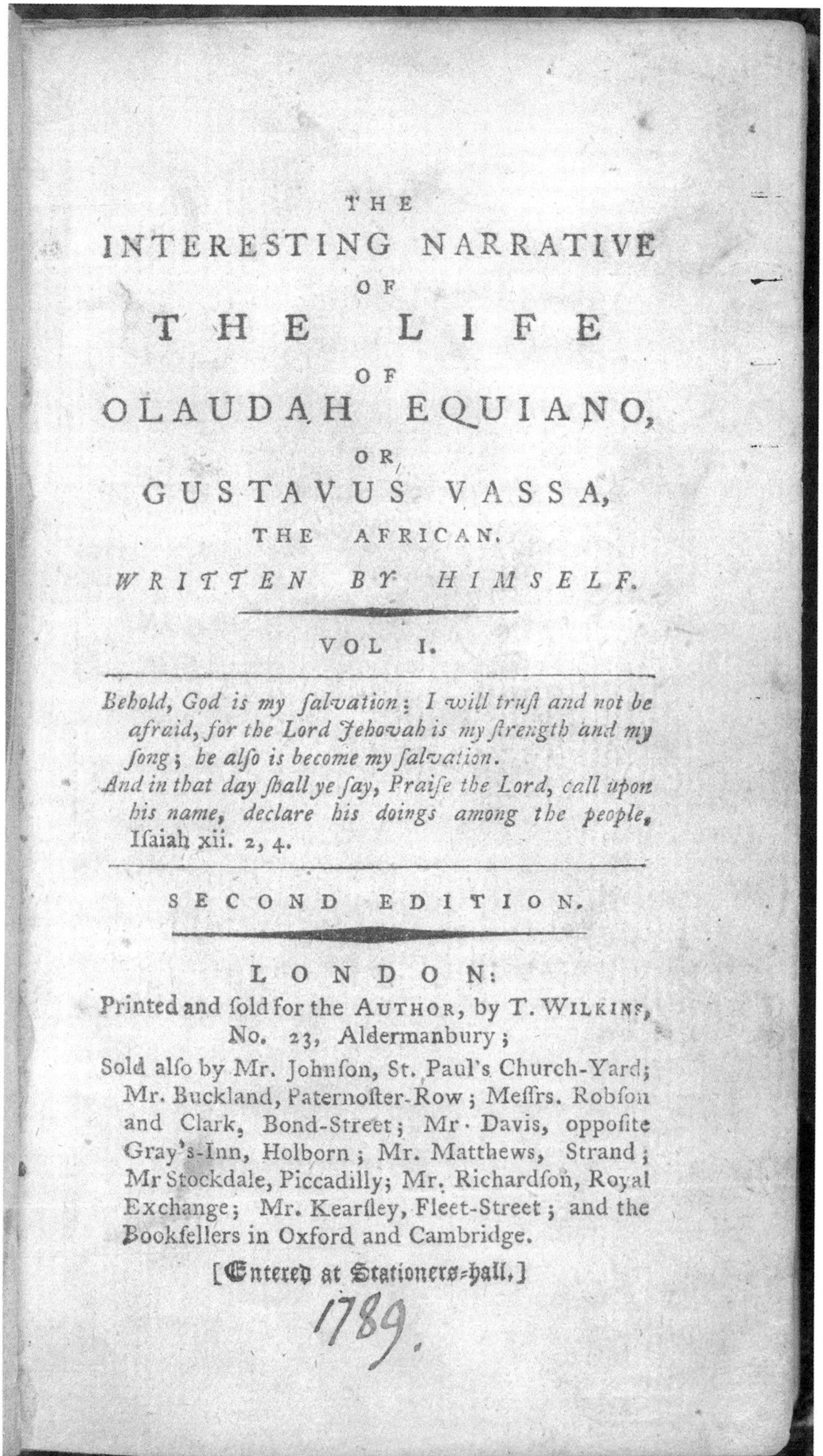

THE

INTERESTING NARRATIVE

OF

THE LIFE

OF

OLAUDAH EQUIANO,

OR,

GUSTAVUS VASSA,

THE   AFRICAN.

WRITTEN   BY   HIMSELF.

VOL I.

*Behold, God is my salvation: I will trust and not be
afraid, for the Lord Jehovah is my strength and my
song; he also is become my salvation.
And in that day shall ye say, Praise the Lord, call upon
his name, declare his doings among the people.*
Isaiah xii. 2, 4.

SECOND   EDITION.

LONDON:
Printed and sold for the AUTHOR, by T. WILKINS,
No. 23, Aldermanbury;

Sold also by Mr. Johnson, St. Paul's Church-Yard;
Mr. Buckland, Paternoster-Row; Messrs. Robson
and Clark, Bond-Street; Mr. Davis, opposite
Gray's-Inn, Holborn; Mr. Matthews, Strand;
Mr Stockdale, Piccadilly; Mr. Richardson, Royal
Exchange; Mr. Kearsley, Fleet-Street; and the
Booksellers in Oxford and Cambridge.

[Entered at Stationers-hall.]

1789.

Figure 15.3a   Original frontispiece of Olaudah Equiano's *The Interesting Narrative of
the Life of Olaudah Equiano, or Gustavus Vassa, The African, written by himself,* 2nd edn,
London, 1787. Photo: The British Library

Figure 15.3b   Portrait of the author, Olaudah Equiano,1789. Photo: The British Library

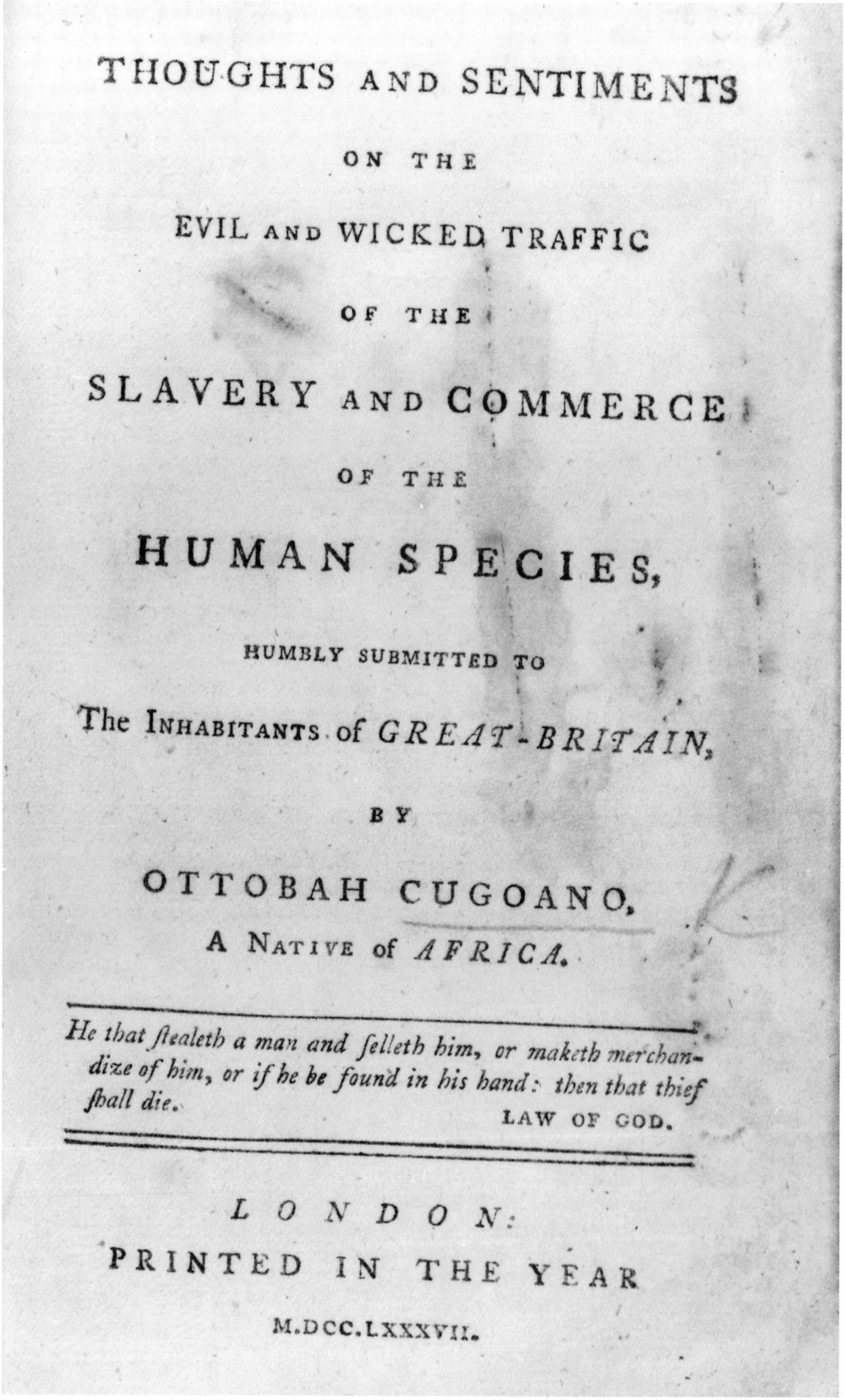

THOUGHTS AND SENTIMENTS

ON THE

EVIL AND WICKED TRAFFIC

OF THE

SLAVERY AND COMMERCE

OF THE

HUMAN SPECIES,

HUMBLY SUBMITTED TO

The INHABITANTS of GREAT-BRITAIN,

BY

OTTOBAH CUGOANO,

A NATIVE of AFRICA.

He that stealeth a man and selleth him, or maketh merchandize of him, or if he be found in his hand: then that thief shall die.   LAW OF GOD.

LONDON:

PRINTED IN THE YEAR

M.DCC.LXXXVII.

Figure 15.4   Ottobah Cugoano, *Thoughts and Sentiments on the Evil and Wicked Traffic of the Slavery and Commerce of the Human Species, humbly submitted to the Inhabitants of Great Britain*, London: T.Becket, etc., 1787, frontispiece. Photo: The British Library

Beliefs and ideologies motivate social actors but they are rarely the effective causes of large-scale historical change; anti-slavery sentiment was no exception. It had captured the moral high ground by the later eighteenth century, but without making the slightest impact on the market transactions that delivered African slaves to the Americas, and slave-grown commodities to Europe. Nor had anti-slavery sentiment effected any change in the legal and political conditions that ensured these transactions were entirely legitimate, and widely lauded as in 'the nation's interest'. Its solitary achievement was to wring from a reluctant Lord Chief Justice Mansfield, in 1772, a clarification of the law respecting the right of a 'servant' to refuse forcible deportation from England. In the famous case of the absconded slave James Somerset, Mansfield ruled that there were no grounds in common law entitling Somerset's owner to force him to return to the West Indies. Mansfield did not unambiguously rule that slavery was incompatible with English law, though his judgement was generally construed in this sense. In France, there was a complete disjuncture between the anti-slavery ideology of the intellectuals and the efflorescence of colonial slavery. Slave imports into the French Antilles were never higher than in the early years of the French Revolution.

THE ST DOMINGUE REVOLUTION

On 22 August 1791, towards the close of the harvest season, an enormous slave revolt broke out in the vicinity of Le Cap (or Cap Français), the main town of St Domingue's northern plain (see Figure 15.5). Slaves armed with machetes and beating drums roamed from plantation to plantation, killing, looting and burning the cane fields. Initially, at least, they were responding to

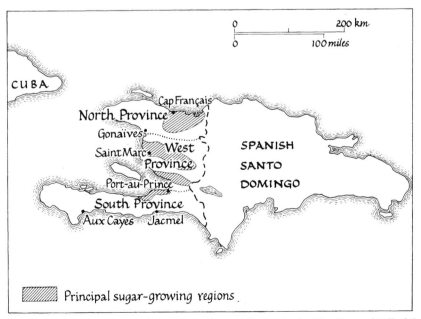

Figure 15.5   Map of St Domingue, 1790, from Philip D. Curtin, *The Rise and Fall of the Plantation Complex*, Cambridge: CUP, 1990

an organised conspiracy directed by elite Creole slaves. There are few undisputed facts about the prelude to the Haitian revolution, but it is generally accepted that the revolt's leaders met in the previous week to plan the uprising and take a blood oath. By the end of September, over 1,000 plantations had been destroyed, hundreds of whites killed, and tens of thousands of slaves had formed themselves into guerrilla bands. It was the largest and bloodiest slave revolt yet seen in the Americas.

What were the causes and pre-conditions for this uprising? *Large-scale* slave rebellions were rare events: in US history, there were many slave conspiracies but only one slave revolt involving more than 100 slaves. Some scholars have located the St Domingue rebellion in a rising tide of maroon resistance, but the evidence for this interpretation is rather slight. In the preceding decades, St Domingue's slaves had been more quiescent than Jamaica's: although individual slaves frequently absconded, incidents of *grand marronage*, when escaped slaves formed communities that threatened planter power, were relatively few in the 1770s and 1780s. Moreover, maroon bands concentrated on the border with Spanish Santo Domingo, many miles from the revolt's epicentre on the northern plain. We may be on firmer ground in emphasising the revolt's *African* origins: huge slave imports before 1791 meant the rank-and-file insurgents were predominantly African-born young men. The revolt's organisation, and its leadership and emotional inspiration, owed much to African religious practices and beliefs. The man who gave the signal for the uprising – known to the French as Boukman – appears to have been the cult leader of a religious sect of a type ancestral to modern Haitian vodou (the preferred spelling).

However, the most important pre-condition for the revolt lay in the internecine struggle among *slave owners*, following the summoning of the estates general in 1788, which had undermined the structure of planter power.[13] The French colonies had not existed when this body last met and, unlike English colonies, had not developed legislative assemblies of their own. They were ruled in absolutist fashion by royal governors and officials. Summoning the estates general triggered an increasingly vicious contest over the right to political representation among the free populations of the French Antilles.[14] St Domingue's complex racial and social hierarchy, and its size and geographic diversity, made for a many-sided struggle, which no group could win single-handedly. The 30–40,000 white residents were divided on lines of social class and inherited privilege between a planter and merchant elite (the *grands blancs*, often from noble families) and an amorphous group of *petits blancs*, or poor whites, mostly estate employees, clerks, artisans and petty traders. Royal officials formed a third white group, deeply resented by Creole planters because they operated the *exclusif*, which denied them lucrative trade with

---

[13] The desperate financial crisis of the French state compelled the monarchy to summon the estates general, which had not met since 1615.

[14] Limits of space preclude considering Guadeloupe and Martinique.

foreigners, prohibited slave imports on foreign vessels (though many were smuggled in from the British Caribbean) and sacrificed their interests to those of metropolitan merchants.

Whites found some common ground in denying legal and civil equality to the roughly equal number of *gens de couleur* ('people of colour') who were nearly all of mixed race and had been formally manumitted or enjoyed de facto freedom. (The tiny numbers of free blacks were also classed as *gens de couleur*. The term 'mulatto' was often applied to the group as a whole, though strictly a mulatto was the offspring of a white and a black parent.) The economic standing of 'people of colour' in St Domingue was quite diverse: most were artisans or small traders, but they included substantial landowners who had been educated in France and were culturally indistinguishable from the white elite. About one in five slaves were owned by 'people of colour'. But whatever their wealth, the social standing of non-whites was uniformly subservient. Anyone with a trace of black ancestry was banned from public office and the professions, and forbidden to wear fine clothing, to carry weapons in town, or to sit with whites in church, at the theatre or when eating. Non-whites were, however, the main source of recruits for the militia and the *maréchaussée* (the rural police). A significant number had served in the volunteer legion sent to aid the rebellious colonists during the American War of Independence.

Whites responded to the coming of the French Revolution by clamouring for political liberty, representation and autonomy, but without conceding an iota to the free coloureds' demand for equality. In 1789, wealthy absentee planters in Paris and resident planters in St Domingue met secretly to elect deputies and ensure their representation in the National Assembly. In early 1790, a Colonial Assembly was convened in St Marc (see Figure 15.5) which declared itself sovereign and drew up a constitution that greatly restricted metropolitan control over trade and administration. Some radical deputies – profoundly influenced by the ideological example of the American Revolution – openly discussed the idea of independence. Meanwhile, *gens de couleur* resident in France had been lobbying sympathetic deputies for a legislative proclamation that would extend citizens' rights to all freemen, whatever their colour. In March 1790, the National Assembly issued a decree on the colony's Constitution, which scrupulously ignored the question of slavery, but included a clause granting the vote to all men over 25 who fulfilled a property qualification. When it reached the Colonial Assembly in St Marc, outraged white colonists swore they would never grant political rights to a 'bastard and degenerate race' and launched a campaign of intimidation against the mulattos. In the autumn of 1790, a notable representative of the free coloureds, Vincent Ogé, secretly returned to St Domingue, determined to wrest equality from the whites by a show of force. He recruited a small army of free coloureds in the north and demanded the governor put an end to racial discrimination. Ogé chose his ground badly, refused to recruit any slaves, and was soon routed, but the incident spread panic among the whites and prompted savage reprisals. Ogé and a fellow conspirator were executed by being broken on the wheel.

The news of this judicial barbarity shocked the French National Assembly, where Ogé's eloquence and civility had won many admirers, and brought the colonial question to the forefront of revolutionary politics. On 15 May 1791, the National Assembly declared free coloureds born of free parents equal to whites. This was not much more than a symbolic gesture of racial solidarity, but after the declaration crossed the Atlantic it prompted a violent white backlash and incipient race war among St Domingue's free population. When the governor – bowing to white pressure – announced he would not promulgate the decree, leading mulattos in the west and south (where they outnumbered whites) formed armed bands to fight for their rights. Whites in mulatto-dominated areas were compelled to seek refuge in the larger towns. Vulnerable mulattos were massacred by white mobs. The white planter elite talked openly of secession. But whites themselves were increasingly factionalised between politically radicalised 'patriots', who sported the revolutionary tricolour, and conservative monarchists, who wore the white cockade.

EXERCISE

This must be a bewildering narrative, and I suspect you require pause for thought. From what has been said so far, summarise the relationship between the French Revolution and the slave uprising.

SPECIMEN ANSWER

The key point is that the slaves rose as the structures of slave-owning power were dissolving into near anarchy. The solvent was the Revolution, which had 'over-determined' events in St Domingue. It was not a direct cause of the slave uprising but it was a *necessary background condition*.

Were the slave insurgents 'revolutionaries'? Objectively, perhaps, in that they were pulverising a socio-economic order, but not consciously: as far as we know, in the autumn of 1791, none were inspired by the French Revolution's ideals. In fact, the revolt's leaders tended to identify themselves as 'black royalists' because they claimed that the 'revolutionaries' in St Domingue's Colonial Assembly had suppressed a royal emancipation edict. Proclamations issued by the insurgents were usually 'in the name of the Church and King' (Geggus, 2002, p. 12). The uprising stalled when its instigator, Boukman, was captured and executed, and its leadership fell to Jean-François and Georges Biassou, who proved themselves capable military commanders, able to hold together their poorly armed and malnourished followers in remote camps. But they had no conception of a revolutionary overthrow of the colonial regime and had an ambivalent attitude to slavery as such. When, in December 1791, negotiations opened between metropolitan commissioners sent to restore order and the insurrection's leaders, the latter were willing to oversee the return of the insurgent mass to bondage provided their own freedom and that of a few hundred elite followers was guaranteed. With crass ineptitude, the white elite in the Colonial Assembly disdained this offer.

At the turn of 1791–2, few could have predicted that within two years slave emancipation would be proclaimed in the regions of the colony under the commissioners' control or that black armies led by former slaves would be major powers in the land. The insurgent slaves faced desperate problems: few knew anything of modern weaponry or military tactics; they were poorly fed and barely clothed; and the African-born were sharply divided by language and ethnicity. Once the commissioners had imposed a measure of unity on white and mulatto forces, and could dispose of French troops, the slave rebellion was fairly easily contained; thousands deserted the slave encampments and sought to return to the security of the plantations. So what determined the sequence that led to emancipation and the irruption of black military power? Part of the answer is that a core of slave insurgents remained at large in the hills and frontier zone; and we should note they found a leader of genius in Toussaint Bréda, better known as Toussaint Louverture ('Opening') (see Figure 15.6). But the overriding factors were the radicalisation of the French Revolution and the outbreak of international war.

The commissioners charged with restoring metropolitan authority in St Domingue, Léger-Félicité Sonthonax and Etienne Polverel, were Jacobins who imported into St Domingue a profound fear of counter-revolution. This was well founded with respect to the white elite: as the Revolution in France became virulently anti-monarchical, the *grands blancs* saw the restoration of the *ancien régime* as essential for the revival of their fortunes and social power. Some thousands of white colonists, who had been driven from their properties either by the slaves or the mulattos, took refuge in Spanish Cuba and Louisiana, and the British West Indies (see Figure 15.1 at the beginning of the unit). Like the noble émigrés who fled across France's borders in 1790, they plotted to invade St Domingue with foreign aid. The news of the declaration of the republic inspired the commissioners to destroy those institutions which might harbour royalist reaction: they dissolved the Colonial Assembly, local municipal bodies, white political clubs, and imprisoned or deported royalist officers and suspect planters. In their stead, they elevated the mulattos to the status of a new ruling class by giving them public office and command of the national guard.

The French declaration of war on the neighbouring colonial powers, Britain and Spain, in January and March 1793, accelerated the destruction of the white community, the transfer of power to the mulattos and the piecemeal emancipation of slaves. The endemic violence undermined slaveholding; as planters fled their properties, slaves turned themselves into squatters. Half the French soldiers sent to secure republican rule in the colony in 1792–3 died from disease within twelve months, so republican officials were compelled to recruit blacks – who were usually promised their freedom – to defend the colony against British and Spanish invaders. One stronghold of white colonists' power was eradicated when the commissioners unleashed slave prisoners and insurgents on Le Cap in June 1793. The occasion was the arrival of a new governor, who had property in St Domingue, and was believed to be sympathetic to the white counter-revolutionaries. Sonthonax attempted to arrest the new governor but was driven out by a white mob. In riposte, he issued a decree promising slave insurgents in the hinterland of Le Cap their freedom if

they 'would fight for the Republic under the orders of the Civil
Commissioner'. It was an invitation to sack the town, which they duly did.
About 10,000 white refugees sailed for the USA. Sonthonax finally decreed
general emancipation on 29 August 1793, when a British invasion was
imminent. He hoped to transform the emancipated slaves into wage-serfs: tied
estate workers compelled to perform paid labour. But the decree disrupted
plantation discipline and encouraged black assertiveness. There is little
evidence that the projected coerced labour system became a reality.

As well as rallying the slave masses to the republican cause, the decree was
intended to win over the black insurgents in the north and east, but it did not
have that effect. When the Spanish invaded from Santo Domingo in May 1793,
the main rebel leaders, Jean-François and Biassou, allied with Spain, as did
Toussaint somewhat later. They were offered freedom, land and grand military
titles in exchange for their services. The French Republic's fortunes were at a
low ebb in the late summer of 1793, and there was reason to believe the
colony would soon be overrun by Spain and Britain. It was not certain that the
French National Convention would ratify Sonthonax's emancipation decree.
Whatever might be true of their followers, the allegiance of the black
commanders was not, in any event, likely to be won by this measure, since
Jean-François and Biassou had sold slave women and children to the Spanish
and had no principled objection to slavery. Toussaint had refused to sell slaves,
which may suggest a principled objection, but the evidence is fragmentary and
conflicting. He was certainly a party to the aborted agreement of December
1791, whereby the insurgent leaders would have returned their followers to
bondage in exchange for securing their own freedom.

Some time in May 1794, Toussaint threw in his lot with the republicans,
although for some weeks he managed to persuade the Spanish that he remained
their ally. This volte-face was to be extraordinarily significant for the course of
the revolution in St Domingue, because – in alliance with the republicans –
Toussaint was to emerge as the colony's supreme ruler. His meteoric rise bears
comparison with Napoleon's, and like Napoleon he exhibited consummate
ability as a military commander, diplomat and political leader. Much is
puzzling about his career, not least his reasons for switching sides in 1794. The
favoured explanation is that he was persuaded to ally with the French on
learning of the National Convention's decree abolishing slavery. C. L. R.
James, the Afro-Caribbean Marxist, made Toussaint the flawed hero of an anti-
colonial epic of social and political emancipation in *The Black Jacobins:
Toussaint L'Ouverture and the San Domingo Revolution* (James, 1989 [1938]).
This is a classic of black history written with great verve and insight, but
archival discoveries have compelled scholars to revise several details in
James's account. We now know that Toussaint had been a freeman for about
twenty years at the time of the slave uprising and that he had rented and owned
slaves. In law, he was an *homme de couleur*. He was a pious Catholic who
spoke his father's African language more fluently than French, which he could
read though barely write. Recent scholars have reinterpreted Toussaint as a
man of the *ancien régime*, indifferent to modern ideology, who sought to

restore the plantation economy and absolutist rule, but under a black monarch and a black plantocracy. As de facto ruler of St Domingue from 1798 to 1802, Toussaint revived the slave trade, outlawed vodou and used corporal punishment to prevent plantation workers leaving to become peasant farmers.

Figure 15.6   Toussaint Louverture (c.1743–1803). Photo: Library of Congress

Very little is known about **Toussaint**'s life before the slave insurrection. He was born on the Bréda plantation in Haut-du-Cap, in the north of St Domingue, given the name Toussaint Fatras-Bâton, and raised as a household slave, not a field hand. He was manumitted in 1776 by a 'private' arrangement which avoided the fees and cumbersome procedures involved in official manumission. In 1779, he became the tenant of a small estate, owned by his son-in-law, to which thirteen slaves were attached. As a freeman and slave owner, he took no part in the early phase of the slave insurrection. The earliest document on which his name appears is an address sent by the insurgents' leaders to the Colonial Assembly in January 1792. In July 1793, after the outbreak of war with Spain, Toussaint was given a command in the forces of Spanish Santo Domingo. He went over to the French side in May 1794, and acquired the soubriquet 'Louverture' ('Opening') after breaking through the Spanish lines on several occasions. The French commissioner, Polverel, exclaimed: 'But this man's creating openings everywhere!' (*Mais cet home fait ouverture partout!*')

Toussaint was made deputy-governor in 1796 and in the following year commander-in-chief of the French forces in the war against the British and their counter-revolutionary allies. His troops, and those of the mulatto leader André Rigaud, forced the British to evacuate the remnants of their expeditionary force (the largest yet despatched from Britain) in August 1798. Soon, the 'aristocracy' of black military officers and mulatto leaders had fallen out over who would be the new masters in St Domingue. By mid-1800, Toussaint had destroyed Rigaud's forces, compelled the leading French officials to return to France, and had brought St Domingue close to independence.

A crucial factor in his rise to undisputed power had been Britain's naval mastery of the Atlantic and Caribbean, which prevented the large-scale reinforcement of republican forces in St Domingue from France. Toussaint's fall from power resulted from the signing of the Peace of Amiens between Britain and France in 1801, and the assent given by Britain in October to a French invasion of St Domingue. Like Napoleon Bonaparte, Toussaint had appointed himself ruler for life in the summer and introduced a constitution that virtually declared St Domingue an independent state. Napoleon had married into a Creole family and had long been pressed by former planters, colonial merchants and officials to mount an expedition that would bring the upstart black to heel. What finally decided the issue was Toussaint's annexation of neighbouring Santo Domingo, where France was now the sovereign power. Led by Napoleon's brother-in-law, General Leclerc, a large French force landed in February 1802, the healthiest month for Europeans to campaign in St Domingue. The aim was to remove the black military aristocracy, restore the plantations to their former owners and institute estate serfdom. Some black commanders cooperated with Leclerc, but Toussaint and Jean-Jacques Dessalines, his principal lieutenant, retreated into the mountains, fighting a bitter rearguard action until compelled to surrender in May. Initially, Leclerc appeared willing to tolerate the black leader's presence, provided he retired to private life, but Toussaint was kidnapped and deported to France in June (with the connivance, it must be said, of Dessalines and other black generals). He died of maltreatment in a French gaol in April 1803, one of the most renowned men in the western world.

Whether Leclerc could have permanently restored French control is debatable, since yellow fever was now ravaging his forces and, fearing the return of slavery, blacks were deserting the plantations and forming guerrilla bands. On 4 July, he wrote to the minister of Marine: 'I entreat you, send me some troops. Without them I cannot undertake the disarming of the population, and without the disarming I am not master of this colony' (quoted in James, 1989 [1938], p. 336). Some days later, Leclerc was shocked to learn that the consular regime in France had restored slavery and the legality of the slave trade in the colonies with the decree of 19 May 1802. The racial discrimination of the *ancien régime* was also revived: 'people of colour' were prohibited from entering France, mixed marriages were banned and sanction given to renewed discrimination against mulattos in the French Antilles. Leclerc's instructions had not included the re-imposition of black slavery and he had repeatedly proclaimed that the Republic would respect black freedom. That commitment was essential to his pacification strategy.

EXERCISE

Read Anthology Document 4.7, 'Letters of General Leclerc to Napoleon Bonaparte, August 1802', and summarise the impact that news of the May decree had on the French position.

Spend about 30 minutes on this exercise.

SPECIMEN ANSWER

Leclerc's pacification strategy was completely undermined. His 'moral force' had been destroyed; henceforth, he could rely only on brute force and that was weakening by the day because of disease in his army. The resistance of the black insurgents had become fanatical.

Along with so many of his men, Leclerc died of yellow fever (and in despair) in early November. As his letters make clear, he relied on black and mulatto generals to hunt down insurgent bands. Before he died, the generals had turned against the French, accepted the overall leadership of Dessalines, and were providing the black insurgency with the military leadership it so desperately needed. Leclerc had resorted to indiscriminate terror; his successor, Rochambeau, openly waged a war of genocide against the black and mulatto population (Geggus, 2002, p. 26). The carnage was ended only by the resumption of war between France and Britain in May 1803, which led to the renewal of the naval blockade and prevented the despatch of further reinforcements. Napoleon had already sent 44,000 troops to St Domingue; in November, the remains of the French army were evacuated. Dessalines inaugurated the independent republic of Haiti on 1 January 1804. It was only the second modern state formed in the western hemisphere, and perhaps the first example of a post-colonial African state.

Haiti was to have an ambiguous relationship with New World slavery. For blacks, it became a symbol of resistance and a haven for refugees and absconding slaves, but the destruction of Europe's richest slave colony gave a great boost to the extension of the plantation system elsewhere. The white and mixed-race planters who fled the violence took their skills and what capital they had to virgin soils: the Louisiana sugar industry was founded by St Domingan refugees; Cuba's coffee and sugar plantations were given a great fillip by the arrival of French planters and technicians, who built all the biggest sugar mills.

In Europe and North America, the Haitian revolution cast a pall over the concept of black or African self-government, not least because Dessalines ordered a massacre of all remaining whites in 1805. For much of the nineteenth century, Haiti was a pariah state: an awful warning of where slave emancipation might lead, and an embarrassment to the emancipationist cause. France refused to recognise Haiti until 1825, when it did so only after securing a massive indemnity for the destruction of French property. Until then, the French had organised an international boycott, which stifled Haitian trade. Haiti was not invited to the first congress of American states held in Panama in 1826 and not recognised by the USA until after the civil war; the idea of black diplomats doing the rounds in Washington was unthinkable while the 'peculiar institution' of slavery flourished south of the Potomac.

THE ABOLITION OF THE ATLANTIC SLAVE TRADE

Britain and the USA were not the first states to outlaw the slave trade: that accolade goes to Denmark, which prohibited Danish participation in the trade and the importation of slaves into the Danish West Indies in 1792, though the law allowed for a ten-year period of adjustment. As we have seen, the French Revolution outlawed the trade. But British abolition inevitably had greater immediate and long-term consequences for the simple reason that British slavers dominated the trade in the early 1800s. *Why* the legislators enacted the measure *when* they did are questions that have long intrigued historians. One answer is simply religiously inspired altruism. People certainly believed this at the time: the royal duke of Gloucester voted for the Bill in the Lords because:

> This trade is contrary to the principles of the British constitution. It is, besides, a cruel and criminal traffic in the blood of my fellow-creatures. It is a foul stain in the national character. It is an offence to the Almighty. On every ground therefore on which a decision can be made; on the ground of policy, of liberty, of humanity, of justice, but, above all, on the ground of religion, I shall vote for its immediate extinction.
>
> (Quoted in Clarkson, 1968 [1808], vol. 2, p. 571)

EXERCISE

Let us, for the moment, credit such men as the duke of Gloucester with meaning what they said; what are the problems of attributing the abolition of the slave trade simply to altruism?

Send about 15 minutes on this exercise.

SPECIMEN ANSWER

There is obviously a problem of explaining the timing. Abolitionists had occupied the moral high ground since the 1780s; their society had been active since early 1787. Why had it taken twenty years to persuade the parliamentary elite that abolition was a moral imperative? Then there is the problem of explaining how altruism came to be reconciled with the national interest.

DISCUSSION

It should not surprise you to know that the West India 'interest' had presented parliament with a wealth of evidence that abolition would subvert the plantation economy, damage British trade and play into the hands of foreign competitors. No body of legislators could lightly ignore such special pleading; even if we accept that altruism ultimately prevailed, we need to explain how and why the trade's apologists were marginalised.

The USA's virtually contemporary abolition of the slave trade highlights the difficulties of explaining abolition in altruistic terms. In the 1760s and 1770s, the Virginia legislature had sought to restrict the external trade, but not out of any sympathy for its victims. The legislature was dominated by slaveholders who feared their slaves would depreciate in value as a result of a glut of imports. One bone of contention between Britain and the colonists was that they were not allowed to regulate the trade in their own interest. When the USA was constituted, Congress was explicitly given the authority to prohibit the international slave trade, though as a concession to the newer slave states, the implementation of the ban was postponed for at least twenty years. The southern slaveholders supported the ban, provided there was no prohibition on the internal movement of slaves to new territories. The House passed the 1807 Bill with only five dissentients because just about everybody agreed that depending on imported Africans for labour was a source of national weakness; neither the legitimacy of slavery nor its control by the individual states was impugned.

EXERCISE

Hindsight inevitably tempts us to see abolition as a step towards emancipation; why is that a mistaken view with respect to the British Act?

Spend about 10 minutes on this exercise.

SPECIMEN ANSWER

As we already know from *Breaking the Chains*, William Wilberforce, the Act's parliamentary sponsor, explicitly denied any intention to emancipate the slaves in the British colonies. Ending slavery – he said – had never been the purpose of the abolition movement; this was a calumny put about by its opponents.

DISCUSSION

Rest assured that Wilberforce is accurately reported in the programme. In his case, the altruistic step of ending the trade has to seen against an ideology of Christian paternalism: slaveholding was not wrong provided masters observed their duty of care and slaves observed their duty of obedience. At this stage in his life, Wilberforce did not believe in an inalienable right to freedom.

Let us revert to the problem of timing. Viewed against the *longue durée* of human history, and in a broad comparative framework, it is rather striking that slave trading and slavery disappeared as quickly as they did in Euro-American societies and colonies. Anti-slavery – a principled objection to human bondage – was a modern and peculiarly western phenomenon; we find nothing comparable in other civilisations. But viewed from the perspective of Thomas Clarkson, composing his *History of the Rise, Progress, and Accomplishment of Abolition of the Atlantic Slave Trade by the British Parliament* immediately after the event, it felt like an awfully long slog.

EXERCISE

Turn to Anthology Document 4.8, 'Thomas Clarkson and the abolition movement', which contains edited extracts from Clarkson's *History*, and read from the beginning as far as paragraph 7. In these extracts, Clarkson explained why the society formed in May 1787 made abolition of the slave trade, not slave emancipation, its objective. Was it because the core members shared Wilberforce's view? (He was not a member of the committee and had not played any part in setting up the society.) What practical measures did the committee take to advance its aims? We have a modern term for bodies such as this, and the sort of politics in which they engage; what is that term? How, in general, do they work?

Spend about 1 hour on this exercise.

SPECIMEN ANSWER

Clarkson makes quite clear that the ten committee members who fixed on abolition as the society's aim were convinced that slavery itself was evil. Slaves were 'deprived of the rights of men ...'. So the committee did not identify with Wilberforce's conservative Christian paternalism; it debated whether its aim should be abolition or emancipation. It settled on abolition partly in the belief that cutting off the external supply would compel planters to improve the lot of their slaves by encouraging marriage and in other ways. Equally, it saw abolition as the more politically feasible objective: it would not interfere with the planters' property rights, and the regulation of trade with colonies was generally accepted as within the competence and the power of the metropolitan government. The committee took two practical steps: the first was to devote some of its funds to the production of *publicity material* in the form of a short pamphlet, written by Clarkson: two thousand copies were to be printed and circulated among subscribers. Second, it authorised Clarkson to *gather evidence* that could be submitted to a parliamentary committee of enquiry, which the committee members expected to result from the 'public agitation of the question'. The modern term for a body such as the society, and the way it set about achieving its end, is *pressure group politics*. Pressure groups try to *mobilise public opinion*, which is then brought to bear on legislators.

"Lobbying"

EXERCISE

You should have gathered from *Breaking the Chains* that the abolition movement perfected a particular technique in mobilising public opinion. What was it? What did it imply about the skills and social consciousness of quite ordinary people in Britain? (Read Anthology Document 4.8, 'Thomas Clarkson and the abolition movement', from paragraph 7 to the end in connection with this exercise.)

Spend about 20 minutes on this exercise.

PECIMEN ANSWER

The mass petitioning of parliament. Abolitionist petitions were signed by hundreds of thousands of people, so petitioning implies widespread basic literacy.

As Clarkson makes clear, the society did not initiate petitioning to abolish the trade: ordinary folk in Manchester and elsewhere had taken the initiative. Why? Outside the slaving ports of Liverpool, Bristol and London, the slave trade was not an immediate issue in people's lives. They had to believe that collectively they could make a difference to something happening thousands of miles away and which, ostensibly, did not concern them. Petitioners demonstrated an awareness that the market had created chains of connection between themselves, as consumers, and Africans sold into slavery.

DISCUSSION

The petitioning campaign marked a historic shift in the way public opinion was organised and articulated in Britain. The most intensive petitioning was in Manchester, the industrial boom town of the 1780s and 1790s, which had neither a member of parliament nor a corporate local government. Almost 11,000 men signed its petition, which probably means that two-thirds of adult males, and the bulk of working men, were signatories (Drescher, 1987, p. 201). At this point, women – along with paupers and children – were generally excluded from signing petitions and participating in local abolitionist committees. When solicited for funds, middle- and upper-class women usually contributed to a separate 'lady's subscription'. There were significant exceptions, but abolitionists around 1790 usually considered women signatories would discredit their cause. (You have seen a strong echo of this in Wilberforce's shocked reaction to the part women played in demanding immediate emancipation in the early 1820s.) Petitioning first peaked during 1791–2, when 519 abolitionist petitions, signed by about 400,000 people, were delivered to parliament from all over Britain.

The petitioners initially made little headway with the parliamentary elite. Wilberforce was known to be a sympathiser, and he wielded considerable influence through his connection with the Clapham sect of evangelical Anglicans and his close friendship with the prime minister, William Pitt. But the gulf between Anglican parliamentarians and a movement launched largely by dissenting tradesmen is evinced by the fact that Wilberforce did not join the London Abolition Committee until 1790, and kept his membership secret for a further year.

What made the political class look at the trade in a new light was the evidence – gathered by Clarkson from the muster rolls of 20,000 seamen – that disease mortality among slaving crews was draining the Royal Navy's manpower reservoir and endangering the national interest. In early 1788, after a long interview with Clarkson, Pitt asked a committee of the Privy Council to investigate the trade. The hearings did not augur well for abolition, since in the first month only witnesses interested in continuing the slave trade were summoned. Lieutenant Matthews – whose testimony you encountered in Unit 13 – was a star turn. But Clarkson restored some balance by priming hostile witnesses to appear before the committee. When the trade's apologists rushed into print a pamphlet entitled *Scriptural Researches on the Licitness of the Slave Trade*, he persuaded the Rev. James Ramsay, a prominent abolitionist, to write a rebuttal, which went to every member of parliament. In early May, Clarkson had an interview with Charles James Fox, a leading Whig MP, at which the latter endorsed total abolition.

1788

On 9 May, the House of Commons debated the slave trade for the first time and resolved to set up its own investigative committee in the next session. Shortly after the debate, Sir William Dolben introduced a measure to limit the number of slaves that could be carried per ton on a slaving vessel and to provide bounties for captains and surgeons on slaves landed alive in the Americas. The Liverpool slave merchants petitioned angrily against Dolben's Bill and Lord Chancellor Thurlow denounced it in the House of Lords as a gross interference with legitimate trade that would hugely advantage French competitors. Pitt threatened to break up the ministry if the measure did not become law, which it duly did.

Between the summer of 1788 and April 1791, when an abolition motion was eventually debated, the abolitionists and the slave trade's supporters both sought to dominate the proceedings of the Commons committee and win over uncommitted parliamentarians. Sixty abolition witnesses were mustered and an abstract of evidence produced astonishingly quickly in the autumn of 1790 and distributed to all MPs. Unfortunately, the abolition motion was put as the conservative reaction to the French Revolution and political radicalism in Britain was growing: it was defeated in the Commons by 163 votes to 88. As with *all* slave trade motions, the majority of MPs did not vote, let alone participate in the debate.

Wilberforce introduced a second abolition motion in April 1792. In his lengthy speech, he did not deny that he desired the emancipation of the slaves. 'But, alas, in their present degraded state, they were unfit for it! Liberty was the child of reason and order.' It could not flourish 'in unrestrained licentiousness.' He alluded to Denmark's 'noble example' as an encouraging sign that other nations would abandon the trade. In the ensuing debate,[15] several speakers referred to the St Domingue rebellion, but not all were apologists for the trade; in a brilliant speech, Fox asked whether any more weighty argument could be produced in favour of abolition than the horrible scenes in St Domingo. Pitt spoke long and cogently for the motion; you may be surprised to learn that the authorities he cited in support of abolition included Edward Long, the historian of Jamaica. He confessed that the civilisation of Africa 'was near his heart ... the present deplorable state of that country ... called for our generous aid, rather than justified any despair, on our part, of her recovery ...'. He concluded his speech at about six in the morning after an all-night sitting. The Commons voted by 230 to 85 in favour of an amended motion for gradual abolition. A subsequent motion proposed the immediate cessation of the trade to foreign ports and the termination of the rest of the trade by 1800; by 151 to 132, the Commons compromised on 1796.

---

[15] The speeches are fully reported in Clarkson (1968 [1808]) vol. 2, pp.355–448.

XERCISE

So why did abolition not become law before the end of the century? (Think of an essential step in the passage of any national legislation.)

Spend just a few minutes on this exercise.

PECIMEN ANSWER

The Bill had to get through the Lords, who deferred it in favour of their own investigation of the slave trade.

The outbreak of war eroded support for abolition in the Commons and made it a less popular cause in the country. Wilberforce introduced an abolition motion every year between 1795 and 1799 and again in 1802; the most votes he mustered in favour was eighty-three – less than 15 per cent of MPs. His parliamentary support improved with the admission of Irish MPs to Westminster (following the 1801 Act of Union) who were generally hostile to the slave trade. For this reason, the Commons voted for an abolition motion in June 1804, but the measure fell on a technicality before being taken up by the Lords. Many of the Irish MPs then defected, after strenuous lobbying by the West India interest persuaded them that abolition represented a threat to property. In 1805, an abolition motion was again defeated.

At this point, the geo-political realities of a world at war intervened. By 1805, over half the slave trade and half the world's trade in plantation produce were in British hands; their value to British entrepreneurs had never been greater. British capitalists were extending the sugar frontier by shipping slaves to the virgin soils of Trinidad (captured in 1797) and to Dutch Guiana (captured in 1803), but it was far from certain these territories would remain British following any peace treaty. So there was a potential danger of creating future competition for the *established* Jamaican and Barbadian planters, who were enjoying high prices and easy access to European re-export markets. They were not 'footloose' capitalists able to lay their hands on liquid assets and they preferred the security of a market monopoly to the uncertainties of moving capital and labour to new lands on the sugar frontier. They could easily be brought to see the wisdom of prohibiting the slave supply to captured foreign colonies by both British and neutral vessels. No question of interfering with legitimate commerce; it was 'in the national interest'! There was no demur when Pitt banned the trade to captured territories by Order in Council, that is to say administrative decree, and instructed the navy to interdict the neutral trade to enemy territories.

The forming of a new ministry, led by abolitionists of long standing, Fox and Lord Grenville, in February 1806, tipped the scales in favour of complete abolition. It was an uneasy coalition and prohibiting the trade was one of the few things on which contending factions agreed. However, when introducing the Foreign Slave Trade Bill to give statutory force to Pitt's administrative decree, the attorney-general made only fleeting reference to humanity. Among the Bill's supporters, there was a conspiracy of silence as to the humanitarian ideals which had, as a matter of fact, kept them plugging away at abolition for eighteen years. Wilberforce did not speak; the West India interest did not contest the measure; only forty-eight MPs bothered to vote (thirty-five for, thirteen against). The measure was more contentious in the Lords, which had many fewer members than the Commons. Sixty-one peers voted (forty-three for, eighteen against). The peers better sensed the full implications of the Bill than the Commons, but those who gave their assent mostly believed the measure, taken in the national interest, would leave the trade fundamentally intact. *In fact, it brought nearly three-quarters of British slaving activities to an end* (Anstey, 1975, p. 376).

Abolitionists in the ministry and on the backbenches soon secured a motion envisaging the complete closure of the trade, but could no longer plausibly claim to be acting in the 'national interest'. By any calculation, British economic interest lay in maintaining the slave trade to its own possessions while denying it to its enemies and competitors. Total abolition could only be based on the appeal to humanity and justice. Yet, the Foreign Slave Trade Act had broken a log-jam of resistance by massively curtailing hitherto legitimate commerce: since a few dozen legislators had done a good deed for base reasons, it was easier for larger numbers to honour their Christian principles. Although the West India interest and Liverpool merchants put up a stiff rearguard action, focusing their obstructive efforts on the Lords, where the 1807 Act originated, they could not seriously argue that abolition implied immediate ruin. The measure easily passed the Lords, partly because of the unanimous support of the bishops. The vote in the Commons was an overwhelming 282 for, 16 against.

EXERCISE

Re-read this section and assess the relative significance of extra-parliamentary opinion and manoeuvrings within the parliamentary elite in abolishing the slave trade.

Spend about 25 minutes on this exercise.

SPECIMEN ANSWER

This is a thorny problem of historical interpretation to which there is no simple 'correct' answer. I would give greater emphasis to the political process at the parliamentary centre than the mobilisation of public opinion. This was immensely important in putting abolition on the political agenda, but the crucial decisions were taken by elite politicians who were culturally insulated from the great body of petitioners. Revolution and international war, rather than the state of domestic opinion, created the circumstances in which legislators first allowed an abolition measure to fail, then later to enact two which quickly ended the British trade. Of course, there was anti-slavery sentiment in parliament as well as in the country, but parliament also offered a forum for powerful vested interests, who were past masters of procrastination. Humanity and justice were, finally, the grounds on which Lords and Commons voted for complete abolition, and in this they were at one with public opinion. But the tortuous political process by which they reached this decision was located in parliament, especially in the Lords.

I would, however, add an important rider. Once abolition was accomplished, it was impossible for the government of the day to defy public opinion and soften its stance against the slave trade. In 1814, the foreign secretary, Lord Castlereagh, appeared ready to let France resume the trade in order to win other concessions from Louis XVIII at the Congress of Vienna. On short notice, the abolitionists launched a nationwide petition campaign to press for articles against the trade at the peace negotiations. In a little over a month, some 800 petitions with about 750,000 names were gathered. About one in eight adults aligned themselves with the demand for international agreements to end the slave trade (Drescher, 1986, p. 82). Though irritated by this abolitionist pressure, Castlereagh could not ignore it: he felt compelled to seek an international agreement on the slave trade as part of the peace treaty. British governments committed considerable resources – that is, taxpayers' money – to suppressing the traffic. In 1819, a separate Slave Trade Department was established in the Foreign Office to oversee the anti-slaving campaign and the African Squadron was formed to patrol the west coast of Africa. The direct costs of suppression up to 1865 were £12.4 million (Eltis, 1987, p. 93). The indirect costs, which included higher sugar prices at home, may have been around £16 million.

In the short term, abolition had few of the detrimental consequences its opponents feared. The only clear losers were the merchants – based mainly in Liverpool – directly engaged in the slave trade. The West Indian planters and their consignees (or the London merchants who handled their produce and advanced them credit) were not economically disadvantaged, though they had experienced a severe political setback. In 1815, the British West Indies produced about 54 per cent of world sugar exports – a much larger share than in 1790. Before becoming the 'workshop of the world', Britain – thanks to its slave empire – was the world's grocer: the proportion of global plantation produce being sourced by British colonies in 1815 was probably greater than the British share of world manufactured output in 1865 (Eltis, 1987, p. 6).

However, the outbreak of peace soon revealed that abolition seriously affected the capacity of the British Caribbean plantation economy to compete in international markets. Between 1807 and 1833, the combined slave population of the old and newly acquired colonies declined by 14 per cent; the fall was much sharper in what had been Dutch Guiana than in Jamaica, where numbers declined immediately after abolition because of adverse demography, and then grew very slowly. Meanwhile, the slave population of Cuba, which continued to import African slaves and was emerging as a major sugar and coffee producer, expanded rapidly. Planters' labour costs in the British Caribbean rose, relative to their competitors', and their labour supply was insufficient to keep pace with the expansion of global demand for plantation produce. While sugar output increased by about 0.5 per cent a year in the British Caribbean in the two decades after abolition, in Cuba and Brazil it increased by up to 2 per cent a year. Cheap imported slaves explain these different rates of growth. Despite the naval patrols that sought to suppress the Atlantic slave trade, it soon revived after 1815, but since more than half the slave markets in the Americas were now closed, the price of slaves on the African coast was very low. Portuguese, Brazilian and Cuban slavers were now in a buyers' market. See Table 15.1.

Table 15.1   Slave populations in Jamaica and Cuba

Jamaican slave population		Cuban slave population	
1788	226,432	1792	84,590
1800	300,000	1817	199,145
1834	310,000	1827	286,942
		1841	436,495

SLAVE EMANCIPATION IN BRITAIN'S COLONIES

DVD exercise

Breaking the Chains offers an engaging account of emancipation and it should not be necessary for me to narrate the events leading up to the Slave Emancipation Act of 1833. Using the knowledge you have gained from the programme, write brief answers to the following questions. You will also find it useful to look at Anthology Document 4.9, 'Elizabeth Heyrick's call for a total end to slavery'.

1   Most of the campaigners for abolition had emancipation as their long-term goal; why was there a lull in their activities between 1807 and 1823?

2   What were the objectives of the Anti-slavery Society formed in 1823? What sort of people – in terms of their social class and ideology – would have 'signed up' for it?

3   What challenge did the society quickly face from people it would have considered its natural supporters?

4   The programme indicates there was a striking change in slave beliefs and ideology in the twenty years before emancipation; what was it? How did it come about? What other changes in slave demography, culture and social consciousness were taking place in this period? (You will have to think for yourself about this.)

Spend about 40 minutes on this exercise, or more if you need to watch the programme again

SPECIMEN ANSWER

1   The war and immediate post-war years were unpropitious for any popular political activity; emancipation did not become a public issue until the relaxation of government hostility to large-scale voluntary association for political ends. To which we can add that some abolitionists had naïvely expected slave holding to reform itself out of existence when cut off from its African supply.

2   The objectives are indicated by its full title: it was 'The Society for Mitigating and Gradually Abolishing the State of Slavery throughout the British Dominions'. Mitigation meant ameliorating the slaves' condition by the judicial regulation of corporal punishment, the prohibition of Sunday work, and widening opportunities for manumission through self-purchase. Apart from die-hards in the West India interest, just about anyone could sign up for that. The society's president was Prince William Frederick, duke of Gloucester; its vice-presidents included fourteen members of the House of Commons and five peers. The Westminster government itself was pressing the colonial assemblies to ameliorate the slaves' condition.

3   The society soon faced radical critics who demanded immediate emancipation. The most notable was the Leicester Quaker Mrs Elizabeth Heyrick,[16] who published the anonymous pamphlet *Immediate Not Gradual Emancipation* in 1824. (It was subtitled: *An Inquiry into the Shortest, Safest, and Most Effectual Means of Getting Rid of West-Indian Slavery.*) Heyrick argued for a mass boycott of slave-grown produce in the belief that, when deprived of a market for their produce, slave holders would be forced to switch to free wage labour.

4   The striking change was the Christianisation of many slaves as a result of nonconformist missionary work. Methodist missions dated back to the 1780s but became much more active with the outbreak of peace in 1815. For perfectly good reasons, the programme focuses on the Baptist mission of William Knibb, but the Methodists were the more successful denomination in terms of the numbers of converts. Probably four-fifths of slave converts were Methodists. Christianisation encouraged literacy and new forms of association, partly because trusted slave converts were given passes that allowed them to move freely from estate to estate. Chapel congregations were communities of freedom and equality, whatever one's legal status and colour. Black slaves served as deacons – positions of honour and respect. But there were other cultural changes associated with the rapid decline in the proportion of African-born slaves: all were coming to speak the same patois. African religious practice was either disappearing or blending with Christian belief.

EXERCISE

Breaking the Chains represents the Sam Sharpe rebellion of late December 1831, in the Montego Bay area of Jamaica, as the crucial event that compelled the Whig government under Lord Grey to move from a policy of amelioration to one of emancipation. Scepticism is the first virtue of the historian, and as budding historians you will want to know whether the programme's account of the rebellion is authentic. You can make a judgement on this from some contemporary evidence in Anthology Documents 4.10, 'Report on the Sam Sharpe rebellion, and 4.11 'Sam Sharpe rebellion – witness testimonies and confessions from convicted prisoners'. The first piece of (very partial) testimony consists of the report of a committee of the Jamaican House of Assembly into the cause of the rebellion, which was sent to the British government in June 1832 (extracts from the report are given in Anthology Document 4.10). Appended to the brief report were the verbatim record of witnesses examined under oath and the confessions of convicted slaves, some of

---

[16] Sometimes spelt Heyricke.

them under sentence of death (extracts from the witness statements are given in Anthology Document 4.11). These confessions were heard by an Anglican rector, Thomas Stewart, who was scarcely a neutral party: Anglican priests detested the nonconformist missionaries and all their work. So there must be some doubt as to whether the confessions were accurately recorded. Internal evidence suggests to me they were: some are very garbled and confusing, and it is hard to believe that Stewart would have recorded them in this form had he meant to doctor the evidence. Of course, whether condemned prisoners *tell* the truth is another matter. Read through the report and the confessions and judge the authenticity of the programme's account for yourself. Linton's confession will be easier to follow if read last. This is a complex exercise so, rather than giving a specimen answer, I have moved straight on to a discussion.

Spend about 90 minutes on this exercise.

SPECIMEN ANSWER

I would say that, given the constraints of a television narrative, the programme makers have been pretty faithful to the historical record. The Colonial Assembly's report tells us as much about the temper of the beleaguered white Jamaicans as it does about the rebellion. The report considered interference by the Westminster government, coupled with the anti-slavery campaign within and outside parliament, to have been the 'most powerful cause' of the uprising. The slaves, it argued, had been deluded into believing they would be free after Christmas 1831, and had prepared to fight for this freedom if they were denied it. Nonconformist missionaries had, the report asserted, created a leadership of slave malcontents by appointing 'the artful and intelligent' to positions in the chapels. The report then refers to a fourth cause which the programme does not mention (inevitably, given the selective nature of a television narrative). This was 'the public discussions of the free inhabitants' regarding further measures of amelioration. 'Free people of colour' were just under 10 per cent of Jamaica's population in 1832 and considerably outnumbered whites: their demand for civil and political equality was significant in destabilising the racial hierarchy which sustained slave holding. However, the evidence does not indicate 'free coloureds' played a significant role in the rebellion and I don't think the programme can be seriously faulted for ignoring them.

The interrogation and confession of Robert Gardner is, I believe, the most detailed insider's account of the rebellion available to historians. Note that Gardner had never been flogged and claimed to have read the newspapers, which strongly suggests he was an elite domestic slave rather than a field hand. The details of his verbatim evidence vividly confirm the general accuracy of the programme's account up to the outbreak of the rising; Samuel Sharpe did bring newspapers from Montego Bay and read them to the slaves. The slaves did believe the king of England and parliament had given Jamaica freedom, which the whites were holding back. You will have noted that he called Sharp[17] and Tharp, another slave, 'rulers'; I think 'rulers' here means lay leaders in the Baptist chapels. In his signed statement, Gardner was obviously trying to minimise his own role in the conspiracy and to shift all blame onto Sharp's shoulders. In Gardner's account, Sharp is not at all the saintly pacifist portrayed in the programme. You will have noticed that Gardner referred to him as 'General Sharp' – apparently without irony – and that he appeared to exercise some kind of military command over the insurgents, whom

---

[17] The spelling in Gardner's statement; Sharpe is more usual.

Gardner called 'General Sharp's army'. He also referred to 'a regiment of Sharp's, under the command of Captain Johnstone' rushing off to attack the Belvidere plantation and 'different regiments [being] detached to different places'. This strongly suggests that Sharp was coordinating the uprising in military fashion, which is not at all the impression given by the programme. Have the programme makers 'sanitised' Sharp? I leave it for you to judge.

Linton's confession, which was made in the presence of M'Kinley, another slave prisoner, suggests a long-standing intention to stage an uprising ('This business has been providing for for more than two or three years ...'). He names Gardner along with Sharp as 'the chief heads'. According to Linton 'we were all sworn upon the Bible to do our best to drive white and free people out of this country' and the elite slaves were to become the new plantocracy, lording it over the 'common negroes, who were not to get their freedom ...'. Was this true? Why should a man about to be hanged make it up? Whether it was true or not, a television narrative cannot deal with this kind of complexity in the evidence. According to Linton, 'we [the slaves] heard in the newspapers, that the people in England were speaking very bold for us; we all thought the King was upon our side.' But in Linton's account, it was Gardner, not Sharpe, who took the lead in conveying this message. And if his interrogator wished to know more about 'the business' he should 'go and ask Gardner and his friends that advise him ...'. So, apparently, Gardner was the chief conspirator. (Linton was not the only condemned slave to make this allegation: Robert Morrice, in his confession, stated: 'I never heard any one speak of rebellion in our quarter until Robert Gardner came up and put it into our heads'.)

To reiterate, the programme makers have generally been faithful to the historical record. But when we examine the evidence closely we can see that it has been used selectively, to offer a compelling portrait of Sharpe as a devout, non-violent martyr in a noble cause. The truth may have been more complex – and perhaps more interesting; whatever it was, it is difficult to unravel from the conflicting testimony.

Why was Samuel Sharpe's rebellion – assuming that's not a misnomer! – such an accelerator of history? There had been other slave disturbances in the recent past: in Demerara, in August 1823, a few thousand slave insurgents mistook 'amelioration' for emancipation and confronted the governor with a demand for their 'right'. Their protest was mercilessly crushed; about 250 slaves were killed by troops or hanged. A local court sentenced a white missionary, the Rev. John Smith, to death for complicity in the rebellion. The Privy Council commuted his sentence, but he died in gaol before the decision arrived. Smith's fate, and the burning of missionary chapels by mobs of planters, outraged British nonconformity. The events in Demerara prompted Mrs Heyrick to publish a second pamphlet in 1824, in which she contrasted the savagery of the whites with the peaceable resistance of the slaves, whom she portrayed as Christian martyrs. Yet the Demerara events did not accelerate change in the same way as Sharpe's rebellion and its ensuing repression. This was partly a matter of scale: perhaps 20–30,000 slaves were involved in the Jamaican disturbances (though we must note this was less than one in ten of the island's slaves), but more importantly its repressive aftermath reverberated with British politics in 1832 in a way that was simply not possible in 1823–4.

EXERCISE

What had changed in British politics between 1823/4 and 1831/2 to make the aftermath of Sharpe's rebellion so consequential?

Spend about 5 minutes on this exercise.

SPECIMEN ANSWER

A campaign for parliamentary reform had come to dominate British political life and to threaten the established power structure.

DISCUSSION

The intensity of political mobilisation brought Britain to within an ace of revolution in 1831–2, according to Edward Thompson, the greatest historian of the period (Thompson, 1963). The Whig government under Lord Grey came into office pledged to enlarge the franchise: it finally persuaded the Tory-dominated House of Lords to pass the Reform Act in June 1832. Until then, colonial slavery was not a major preoccupation for radical reformers either within or outside parliament; indeed, militant populists – such as William Cobbett – berated the anti-slavery movement for fretting over idle blacks while condoning 'wage slavery' in Britain. However, the Anti-slavery Society – in which Methodists had become increasingly influential – had abandoned its original gradualism; in May 1830, its annual meeting voted in favour of immediate emancipation. Grey's government announced it would have nothing to do with this, though it did agree to press the colonial legislatures to enforce amelioration. The 1832 Act transformed the political terrain for the nonconformists who were now setting the pace in the Anti-slavery Society. We must recall that, before 1828, England was an Anglican confessional state in which the Test and Corporation Acts excluded nonconforming Protestants from public office and, usually, from the electoral rolls. Their righteous anger at events in Demerara in 1823 could be shrugged off by the governing oligarchy because nonconformists were not then legally part of the political nation. Nonconformist outrage at the reign of terror unleashed in Jamaica by the Anglican Colonial Church Union in early 1832, when fourteen Baptist and six Methodist chapels were destroyed, could not be so easily deflected. The 1832 Act made a significant concession to popular sovereignty by increasing the electorate from about 500,000 voters to 813,000 (or about one in seven males). In the first elections held under the Act in December, nonconformists were key 'swing' voters in many contested urban constituencies. The Wesleyan conference had been enjoining each congregation to make petitioning for emancipation a religious obligation; in the general election, it urged Methodists to support only those parliamentary candidates who pledged themselves to end slavery immediately. Almost 200 did so. When parliament reconvened, it was inundated with emancipation petitions, signed by over one and half million people, twice the number who had voted in the elections. Even before their outcome was known, the Grey government committed itself to an emancipation measure. A special cabinet committee was appointed to negotiate with the West Indian lobby (which was now seeking maximum compensation for the slave owners, rather than trying to resist the inevitable), the parliamentarians in the anti-slavery movement, and the leading Tories in the Lords. The Emancipation Bill was signed on 28 August 1833 and became operative on 1 August 1834.

Emancipation came at some cost for British taxpayers and consumers. The West Indian interest demanded £20 million compensation for the slave owners as the price for cooperating in emancipation. The government succumbed to this threat and, ignoring the protests of the more radical elements in the Anti-slavery Society, parliament voted what was an astonishingly large sum, in relation to the general level of public spending. The compensation fund represented about 45 per cent of the slaves' total market value and was distributed according to *local* prices. Slave prices were higher in Trinidad and Guiana, so there the owners received more per slave than Jamaican and Barbadian planters. Part of the indemnity came in the form of unpaid labour, which former slaves were compelled to provide the estate owners during their so-called apprenticeship. To help finance the compensation, higher sugar duties were imposed. West Indian planters retained their monopoly on the British market because duties on foreign – invariably slave-grown – sugar were kept at prohibitive levels. The dire warnings of the West India interest that plantation production was not economically viable without slavery proved entirely correct: between 1833 and the late 1840s, the British Caribbean's share of world sugar exports slumped from over one-third to about 12 per cent.

CONCLUSION

This unit has examined contrasting experiences of emancipation: St Domingue's was revolutionary, endemically violent and finally disruptive of the colonial link between Europe and the Americas; the British Empire's was reformist, only sporadically violent and generally strengthened the colonial link. Because Westminster was legislating for a worldwide empire, British slave emancipation had global consequences: it provoked the Great Trek of slave-owning Dutch farmers out of Cape Colony and into what became the independent states of Transvaal and Orange Free State. British plantation islands in the Indian Ocean (principally Mauritius, acquired from France in 1815) were as much affected as those in the Caribbean. The response of colonial legislatures and British officials to the collapse of the slave labour force was to encourage the migration of African and Asian indentured workers: tens of thousands of West African contract labourers were transported to the British Caribbean in the 1840s; similar numbers of *engagés* left East Africa for Indian Ocean plantations. Later in the century, about two million migrant contract workers left South Asia for plantations in Trinidad, Guiana, Natal, Ceylon and Fiji to labour under conditions that were little better than slavery.

Haitian emancipation led to the formation of a weak isolated state; British emancipation was intrinsic to the reformation of Britain as a liberal state at the heart of a liberal empire. In the 1820s, the state had been the class instrument of an Anglican oligarchy; by 1840, the state represented the hegemonic fusion of aristocratic, but increasingly professional, politicians and middle-class men who had made their way in trade, the law and industry. Lord Palmerston and Richard Cobden epitomised this new liberal state. Both hated slavery in the very core of their beings: Palmerston spent more time in his many years in office negotiating with other governments to suppress the slave trade than on any other issue. Cobden felt physically ill when travelling in the southern slave states of the USA. In their background and convictions, these were very different men, but they were united in believing that free labour was the essential basis for a good society.

REFERENCES

Anstey, R. (1975) *The Atlantic Slave Trade and British Abolition, 1760–1810*, Basingstoke, Macmillan.

Blackburn, R. (1988) *The Overthrow of Colonial Slavery, 1776–1848*, New York, Verso.

Clarkson, T. (1968 [1808]) *The History of the Rise, Progress, and Accomplishment of Abolition of the Atlantic Slave Trade by the British Parliament*, London, Frank Cass reprint.

Curtin, P.D. (1990) *The Rise and Fall of the Plantation Complex*, Cambridge, Cambridge University Press.

Drescher, S. (1986) *Capitalism and Slavery*, Basingstoke, Macmillan.

Drescher, S. (1987) 'Paradigms tossed; capitalism and the political sources of abolition' in Solow, B. and Engerman, S.L. (eds) *British Capitalism and Caribbean Slavery: The Legacy of Eric Williams*, Cambridge, Cambridge University Press.

Eltis, D. (1987) *Economic Growth and the Ending of the Transatlantic Slave Trade*, Oxford, Oxford University Press.

Geggus, D.P. (1982) *Slavery, War and Revolution: The British Occupation of Saint Domingue, 1793–1798*, Oxford, Clarendon Press.

Geggus, D.P. (2002) *Haitian Revolutionary Studies*, Bloomington, Indiana University Press.

James, C.L.R. (1989 [1938]) *The Black Jacobins: Toussaint L'Ouverture and the San Domingo Revolution*, London, Allison and Busby reprint.

Thompson, E.P. (1963) *The Making of the English Working Class*, New York, Vintage.

Bernard Waites

Learning outcomes

When you have finished this unit you should:

- understand the value to historians of explicitly comparing social institutions and processes

- have a knowledge and understanding of serfdom in tsarist Russia and chattel slavery in the USA between *c.*1800 and 1860 and be able to compare these systems of coerced labour

- be able to relate serfdom to the formation of the absolutist state in tsarist Russia and slavery to the state formation of the USA

- understand how and why serfdom and slavery were abolished.

INTRODUCTION

This unit compares two systems of bonded labour that persisted in North America and European Russia into the 1860s: chattel slavery and serfdom. The specific questions I will address are:

- What roles did slavery and serfdom play in economic production in the USA and Russia between the 1800s and emancipation in the 1860s?

- How were these institutions legitimised? Slavery in the US south co-existed with the world's most advanced democracy and most legalistic political society. It required a legal framework compatible with the Constitution, but it also had to be defended by politicians, clergymen, newspaper editors and others against increasingly vociferous abolitionist critics in the free states of the north. In other words, slavery needed an *ideology*. Russia was an illiberal state without a formal constitution where political argument was censored. Nevertheless, there was lively discussion of social institutions, which were brilliantly represented in literature. Serfdom had its defenders and detractors and, though ideological arguments were less clear cut and coherent than in the USA, they provide a useful point of comparison.

- How did these institutions intermesh with the state formation of the USA and the tsarist empire?

- Why and in what circumstances were emancipation proclamations issued in Russia in 1861 and in the USA in 1862?

The unit pursues all the overarching themes of A200.

THE HISTORICAL BACKGROUND TO RUSSIAN SERFDOM

Comparative analysis, like travel, broadens the mind and is a good in itself. For historians, it has an instrumental value in revealing underlying patterns of causation in human societies that are not disclosed by narrative accounts focusing on a single country. To take a pertinent example, at roughly the same time, slavery and serfdom were both institutionalised and embedded in the American colonies and on the Russian steppe – regions we can usefully describe as the western and eastern peripheries of an expanding Europe.

As you know, in the manorial economy of medieval western Europe, most agrarian workers were serfs, bound to the land and compelled to render dues (in labour, kind or money) to their lord or seignior. By the seventeenth century, serfs were few in number in the west and their serfdom was vestigial. However, serfdom followed a different historical trajectory in the principality of Moscow, the original core of the tsarist empire. As the institution disappeared in the west, it became more widespread and coercive in the east. In Russia, the imposition of serfdom was closely related the re-formation of the state after the Russian princes shook off what is known in Russian history as the 'Tatar yoke'.[18] Between the mid fifteenth and mid seventeenth centuries, the rulers of Moscow transformed their realm into a patrimonial state and greatly extended its territory.[19] Russia became a gigantic royal domain 'owned' by the tsar: he was the lord, the population his *kholopy* (usually translated as 'slaves'), the land and all else that yielded profit his property (Pipes, 1974, p. 85). In this process of absolutist state formation, commoners who had hitherto been free tenants were incrementally tied to the land and enserfed. By 1650, most peasants (the *muzikhi* or 'little people') had had their freedom of movement restricted and legal rights to own land negated. Serfdom was not formally promulgated, but instituted piecemeal (and with major regional variations) in two lengthy phases: in the first, beginning in the later fifteenth century, peasants were assigned to tracts of land whence they could depart only after fulfilling labour and tax obligations and only at certain times of the year; in the second phase (beginning in the 1590s) the peasants' status was transformed from that of tied labourer to the 'baptised property' of the lords whose lands they tilled. In 1581–92, the population was registered in a series of local cadasters or land surveys, so that in case of dispute a peasant's proper residence could be determined. A system for hunting down serf fugitives and returning them to their masters was instituted. Some peasants

---

[18] Mongol armies conquered Russia and much of eastern Europe in 1236–41. For more than a century and a half, the Russian princes were tributary vassals of the 'Golden Horde', a Mongol–Tatar khanate based on the lower Volga.

[19] The first formally to assume the title tsar – the Russian form of caesar, meaning emperor – was Ivan IV in 1547, though previous rulers had occasionally called themselves tsar. Until the fall of Constantinople in 1453, the grand dukes of Moscow thought of the Byzantine emperor – to whom they owed a shadowy allegiance – as the 'tsar'. In a patrimonial state, the land, its people and all goods are the patrimony or hereditary property of the ruler.

were retained on lands owned by the state and administered by the treasury; from Peter the Great's reign they were known officially as 'state peasants'. But a larger proportion of peasants was assigned to holders of *pomest'ia*, lands granted to minor nobles in exchange for military service – the nearest equivalent is 'fief'. For these proprietorial peasants, serf status became hereditary and inescapable, except by flight to border regions, where the common people remained free, or by twenty-five years' military service.

By the 1600s, serfdom was an economic and social reality, but had yet to be formally systematised in law. In theory, at least, a peasant denied permission to leave his lord's lands by the local seigniorial court (in which his lord was the judge) could appeal to a royal court. From the mid seventeenth century, a series of imperial decrees removed this vestigial right. They both retrospectively sanctioned the appropriation of the serfs by their seigniors, the *pomeshchiki*,[20] and accorded them a legal jurisdiction over agrarian society that virtually excluded the state's judicial system. Except where paid officials directly administered state-owned lands, the state had no direct relations with the peasants. This was not a symptom of the central state's weakness; on the contrary, the serfs' subjection to the *pomeshchiki* provided the social foundations for the absolutism of the autocracy. During the century serfdom was being instituted, all landowners were compelled to serve the rulers of Moscow as military or civilian officials: they remained a service class (or more accurately 'estate', in the sense of a closed and hereditary social order) until finally released from the obligation in 1785, though entering state service continued to be regarded as the norm for noblemen. They lacked the corporate privileges of the nobility in western Europe, but were given a monopoly on land and serfs: until 1861, apart from the clergy, only those registered on the rolls of the service class could hold landed estates and employ serf labour (Pipes, 1974, p. 87). The *pomeshchiki* were personally exempted from taxation, but had to ensure taxes were gathered from serf households.

Why was serfdom being imposed and extended in Russia, when the institution was in advanced decay in western Europe? As I have indicated, the dynamics of enserfment were interwoven with Russian state formation, but is that a sufficient answer? Comparison with the extension of chattel slavery into continental North America suggests not. Both were intended to provide bonded agrarian labour in situations where abundant land and an open frontier made it difficult for landowners to retain free tenants or wage earners. Both slavery and serfdom were associated with the territorial expansion of European commercial agriculture: slaves produced the commodities shipped back across the Atlantic; serfs grew the food for Russia's towns as well as the flax and hemp that were Russia's main exports until about 1840. From the later eighteenth century, when Russia acquired Odessa and other Black Sea ports, the more enterprising *pomeshchiki* began to ship surplus grain to western Europe. Wheat – grown by

---

[20] This is variously translated as 'landowners', 'landlords', 'gentry' and 'noblemen'; 'fief holders' is the most strictly accurate.

serfs in southern Russia – became the principal export in the late 1840s; the trade was given a great fillip when the abolition of Britain's Corn Laws opened up the wealthiest market in the west to agrarian free trade.

Neither slavery nor serfdom was exclusively agrarian: industrial serfdom was instituted in Russia in the 1720s, principally to provide labour for the Urals iron industry. Merchants (as opposed to nobles) were permitted to buy fully inhabited villages for their factories, even to buy serfs running away from their noble masters, so long as their labour remained bound to the factory, not to the present owner. By the end of the century, the leading industrial dynasty – the Demidov family – was employing tens of thousands of serfs in its twenty-nine factories. Slaves worked as factory hands, artisans and labourers in American cities. Around 1850, about 5 per cent of US slaves were industrial workers, probably the same proportion as industrial workers among Russia serfs. Urban slaves usually enjoyed more autonomy than the so-called possessional serfs in the Russian ironworks and mines, who suffered exploitation of an unusually vicious kind, until drastic reforms of industrial serfdom were instituted in the 1820s.

To reiterate, these unfree labour systems were institutionalised quite close in time: the Tsarist Code of 1649, which formalised serf status, was promulgated only a generation in advance of the English colonial statutes that defined and regulated Negro slavery (see the chronology in the *Course Guide*). Comparison of these regulatory instruments demonstrates that the legal status of a Russian serf (though not his or her social or economic condition) was barely distinguishable from that of a slave. Hundreds of articles in the Tsarist Code defined the landlords' power over their peasants, but none set on it any limits, save for the proscription on selling serfs apart from the land to which they were attached. Serfs were not reduced to chattel, but they had to render such dues as the seignior decided, could not leave his estate nor marry without permission, and could not own property in their own right. A male serf required his master's consent to enter holy orders or government service. Serfs were made personally liable for the debts of bankrupt landlords, forbidden to complain against landlords unless state security was involved, and deprived of the right to testify in court in civil disputes (Pipes, 1974, p. 123). In practice, the ban on serf sales was widely ignored: they were sold, mortgaged, exchanged and gambled away with increasing frequency in eighteenth-century Russia. The central government tacitly recognised this by banning the use of the hammer at public auctions of serfs and, in 1833, outlawing the separation of parents and their unwed children by sale or gift (Blum, 1978, p. 41).

serfdom isn't slavery.

Serf owners exercised wide judicial and police powers over their serfs, and only the more heinous criminal offences lay outside seigniorial competence. Landowners could be held to account if they ordered excessive or illegal punishments, but the restraints on their abuse of power became largely theoretical when Catherine II made it a criminal act for serfs to present petitions against their masters, and so stripped them of their only legal resort against mistreatment. Serf owners could not legally kill their serfs, but could have them flogged just short of death. They were probably no more sadistic than any group of men empowered to chastise others physically, but there are countless stories of arbitrary cruelty. One irate owner had a serf's feet held to the fire as a punishment for drowning the puppies his wife had been ordered to breast feed. The direst punishments serf owners could inflict were selecting male serfs for military service – a virtual death sentence – and exiling serfs to Siberia; the novelist Ivan Turgenev recalled that two serfs belonging to his mother suffered this fate because they neglected to bow to her when she passed by while they were working (Blum, 1961, p. 438). In the 1830s and 1840s, the autocracy curbed the serf owners' punitive powers by limiting the corporal punishments they could administer to forty blows with the rod or fifteen with the cudgel and setting a limit of two months to the period in which a serf could be imprisoned in the seigniorial jail (p. 429). A landowner wishing to impose a more severe custodial sentence had to send the culprit to a government house of correction. While the punitive powers of individual serf owners were restricted, the landowning class became more autonomous of the state through the strengthening of a local government system dominated by serf-owning magnates. Most of the administrative and judicial officials charged with supervising the landowners' treatment of the serfs were elected by the local nobility in their triennial assemblies in provincial capitals.

The serf owner was supposed to replicate in the rural localities the paternal authoritarianism exercised by the tsar over Russia as a whole. In 1828, one apologist penned a highly idealised account of the *pomeshchik*:

> I conceive [him] to be a hereditary functionary, to whom the
> sovereign power has given land [and] entrusted stewardship over the
> people there settled. He is the natural protector of these people, their
> local judge, their intercessor, and the guardian of the poor and
> oppressed; he inculcates the good and maintains order and morality.
> (Field, 1976, p. 14)

The consequence of vesting so much authority in the landowners was that, for the great agrarian majority, the state was a remote monolith that rarely impinged on their lives. Rural Russia was under-governed and under-policed. During the revolutionary year of 1848, Nicholas I told a meeting of the nobility of St Petersburg province: 'I have no police, gentlemen; I don't like them; you are my police. Each of you is my steward' (quoted in Field, 1976, p. 15).

Were serfs slaves?

Many late eighteenth-century writers referred to serfs in Russia – and in east central Europe more generally – as slaves. Adam Smith, for example, gave a brief account of 'This species of slavery [which] still subsists in Russia, Poland, Hungary, Bohemia, Moravia, and other parts of Germany' (Smith, (1910 [1776], p. 345). In 1790, an enlightened Russian nobleman, Alexander Radishchev, drew an extended analogy between serfdom and plantation slavery in his *Journey from St Petersburg to Moscow* (Radishchev, 1958 [1790]). The analogy became a commonplace in Russian progressive circles and is echoed by contemporary historians: in the fine comparative study on which I have drawn heavily for this unit, Peter Kolchin writes: 'Russian serfdom must be seen as particular variety of slavery rather than a fundamentally distinct labour system' (Kolchin, 1987, p. 361). I think this is overstated for several reasons

- Even the most oppressed serfs were recognised as legal individuals, who could in certain circumstances initiate and participate in court actions, and who possessed limited rights denied to slaves. Marriage illustrates the presence of legal personality in one case, and its absence in the other: serfs required seigniorial leave to marry and sometimes had to pay a fee; serf girls were often forbidden to marry outside the estate because this would mean the loss of their services, since wives followed husbands. The sexual exploitation of serf women by their owners was commonplace. But serf marriages were sanctified by canon law and anyone violating the marriage was committing an offence. For slaves, marriage and family were simply not legal institutions: the slave unions usually encouraged by American planters had no status in law. A master who raped his female slave committed no crime, unless he sodomised her.

- Serfdom was a more varied condition than slavery. The gulf between the slave minority and free majority could only be bridged by manumission; the boundary between proprietorial serfs and state peasants, who enjoyed greater personal freedom, could be crossed more or less effortlessly. They were socially and culturally identical; both belonged to the peasantry, which meant the overwhelming majority of the Russian population. Servile obligations took two basic forms: either labour dues (*barshchina*) or money payments (*obrok*). A serf household held under *barshchina* customarily worked three days a week on the lord's fields (though with great seasonal variations), which was more onerous than paying a money rent. As well as rendering a labour tribute, serfs had to provide their own horses, oxen and tools, so landowners invested little in farm equipment. By the later eighteenth century, the *barshchina* regime prevailed in the fertile black earth belt of southern Russia where the growing season is longer and agriculture more commercialised. The opening of export markets in western Europe in the early nineteenth century induced landlords to rationalise their estates and exploit serf labour more effectively. The *obrok* regime was more prevalent in central and northern Russia, where agriculture is more precarious. Serfs on *obrok* were often released from their estates to work in towns or in craft workshops, though they had to turn over part of their earnings to their landlords. Serf entrepreneurs founded substantial craft industries; cotton manufacturing in Russia began in this way, for example. There were parallels between *obrok* serfs working in towns and urban slaves in the US south who hired themselves out (and paid their owners a fixed percentage of their income) but the differences in personal status, economic role and social institutions were more significant.

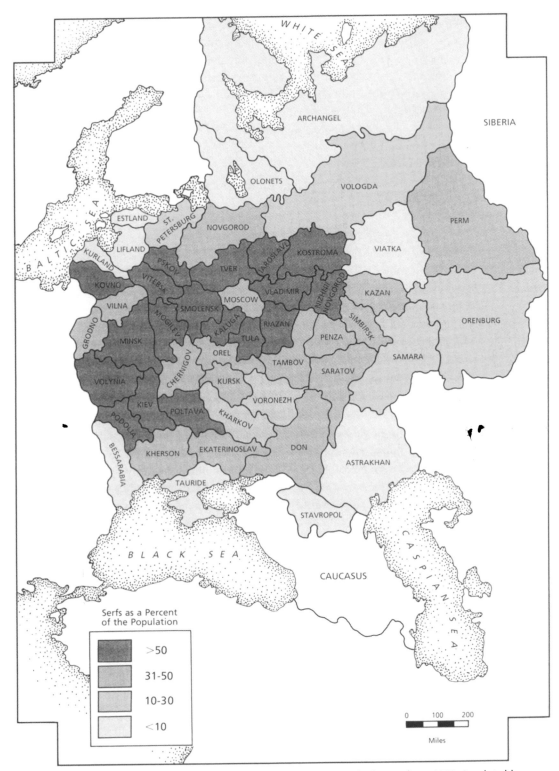

Figure 16.1   Serfs as a percentage of the population in European Russia, by province, 1858. Reprinted by permission of the publisher from Peter Kolchin, *Unfree Labor: American Slavery and Russian Serfdom*, Cambridge, Mass. and London: Belknap Press of Harvard University Press, © 1987 by the President and fellows of Harvard College

- American slave owners practised what we might call 'direct rule' over their slaves. They usually knew them by name and closely regulated their lives. Serf owners ruled indirectly, through the peasant commune or *mir*. The commune was responsible for gathering the taxes which the landowner had to forward to the state and periodically redivided land among serf households.
- Even under the *barshchina* regime, there was no equivalent to the American cotton plantation, the most efficient and profitable form of capitalist agriculture of its day.

Figure 16.1 shows the percentages of the population who were serfs in European Russian provinces in 1858.

SLAVERY AND STATE FORMATION IN THE USA

The Constitution ratified on the 17 September 1787 provided the basic political parameters for the formation of the United States of America: its seven articles sought to ensure the separation of powers between the legislature, executive and judiciary *in the Union*.[21] The representatives of the thirteen states who ratified the Constitution assumed that, unless it specifically vested powers either in Congress or in the federal executive, then these powers remained within the competence of the individual states. This constitutional doctrine was to be crucially significant for the further development of slavery, on which the Constitution was noticeably silent. Section 2 of Article I states:

> Representatives and direct Taxes shall be apportioned among the several States which may be included within this Union, according to their respective Numbers, which shall be determined by adding to the whole Numbers of free Persons, including those bound to service for a Term of Years, and excluding Indians not taxed, three-fifths of all other Persons.

This oblique reference to slaves – who were the 'other Persons' – meant that each slave counted for three-fifths of a person in determining the size of congressional electorates.

Whether or not slavery was permitted was left to the individual states, and it is important to bear in mind that they, too, had been drawing up their constitutions in the preceding years. Massachusetts, Pennsylvania, Rhode Island, Connecticut and Vermont entered the Union as 'free states'; New York and New Jersey passed gradual emancipation laws in 1799 and 1804. The southern states retained a raft of colonial legislation regulating the status of African slaves; some prohibited manumission, others compelled free blacks to leave their territory. It was usually an offence to teach slaves to read and write. The Constitution did not give the Union power to interfere with this

Handwritten margin notes:
7 December
Delaware ratifies the US Constitution + becomes first state of the union.
Pennsylvania + New Jersey follow

21st June 1788
Constitution of US comes into force after its ratification by New Hampshire
then Virginia, NY 1789 (12)
N. Carolina in 1789 (12)
RI in 1790 (13th)

---

[21] The separation of powers was duplicated in the individual states as a result of their constitutions.

legislation, except by the cumbersome procedure for amendments in Article V.[22] However, Section 2, Article IV, states:

> No Person held to Service or Labour in one State, under the Laws thereof, escaping into another, shall, in consequence of any Law or Regulation therein, be discharged from such Service or Labour, but shall be delivered up on Claim of the Party to whom such Service or Labour may be due.

EXERCISE

You may need to re-read this convoluted prose to grasp its import, but basically it meant that a slave fleeing to a free state could not thereby escape slavery. What problems did this provision in Article IV inevitably pose for later generations? Why was this bound to be a source of contention between free and slave-holding states?

Spend about 10 minutes on this exercise.

SPECIMEN ANSWER

There was clearly a problem of *enforcement*. How was a slave owner to enforce his property rights over a slave who had fled to a state jurisdiction where slavery was illegal? To which authority could he turn? And what if a free state passed a law guaranteeing the personal liberty of all its residents, black and white? This raised the problem of *constitutionality* if such a law could be shown to conflict with Section 2, Article IV. Religiously inspired abolitionist sentiment was strong in the north; sympathetic whites could not idly stand by while professional slave catchers attempted to enforce warrants for fugitive slaves in their midst.

Fugitive slaves and US state formation

In 1793, Congress attempted to settle the problem of enforcement with a federal law authorising slave owners to cross state lines to recapture fugitive slaves, whom they were supposed to bring before any local magistrate or federal court to prove ownership. This law denied fugitives the protection of habeas corpus, the right to a jury trial, and the right to testify on their own behalf. In practice, professional slave catchers often abused the law by falsely swearing before the judges that any black captives were the absconded slaves described in the affidavits; not infrequently, kidnapped free blacks were simply spirited south by the quickest route. To counter such abuses, several northern states enacted personal liberty laws, giving fugitives the rights of testimony and trial by jury, and imposing criminal penalties for kidnapping. Northern abolitionists encouraged state officials to use these laws to protect fugitive slaves. In 1837, Pennsylvania convicted a slave catcher, Edward Prigg, of kidnapping after he had seized a slave woman and her children and returned them to their Maryland owner. Prigg's lawyers appealed the case to the US Supreme Court, which, in 1842, ruled the Pennsylvania anti-kidnapping law unconstitutional, upheld the 1793 fugitive slave law and affirmed that a

---

[22] Amendments to the Constitution had to be passed by two-thirds of both houses of Congress *and* ratified by three-quarters of state legislatures.

slaveholder's right to his property overrode any contrary state legislation. But the court also ruled that enforcing the slave owner's rights under Article IV was a federal responsibility, with which the states need not cooperate in any way. This prompted no less than nine personal liberty laws between 1842 and 1850, prohibiting the use of state facilities in the recapture of fugitives. In many northern communities, free blacks and sympathetic whites formed vigilance committees to protect fugitives and obstruct federal marshals attempting to enforce warrants.

In 1850, southerners in Congress secured the passage of a second fugitive slave law, which gave the federal government unprecedented powers to enforce Article IV (see Figure 16.2). There was much irony in this: on every other issue, southerners wanted a weak central government. Under the new law, a claimant could bring an alleged fugitive before a federal commissioner (a new office created by the law) to prove ownership by an affidavit from a slave-state court or by the testimony of white witnesses. US marshals and deputies were bound to help slave owners recapture their property and fined $1,000 if they refused. Stiff criminal penalties were imposed on anyone harbouring a fugitive or obstructing his or her capture. The expenses of capturing and returning a slave were to be borne by the federal treasury. Federal commissioners were given a financial incentive to assist slave catchers: if they found against claimants, they received a fee of $5, but if in favour, $10. The law contained no statute of limitations: claims of ownership were successfully asserted against blacks who had resided in free states for decades. In only eleven cases throughout the 1850s did the commissioners find for blacks brought before them, while 322 fugitives were forcibly returned to slavery. The numbers involved were relatively few, but the abolitionist moral outrage at the spectacle of hundreds of US deputies and soldiers enforcing the fugitive slave law in Boston, and other anti-slavery cities, was enormous. Southerners were equally indignant that whites and free blacks conspired to frustrate the assertion of their property rights and resist the law by sheltering fugitives and helping them escape to Canada. The law exposed an ideological chasm between northern Christians who believed the Constitution should be consistent with divine and natural law, and southern Christians who believed slavery was sanctioned by the Bible and enshrined in Article IV. In the 1850s, all the major denominations split on sectional lines.

The social impact of the fugitive slave law was, by the way, greater than the number of cases under it might suggest, since thousands of free blacks migrated to Canada in the 1850s to escape its consequences. We must, furthermore, bear in mind that only a small minority of abolitionist crusaders – they were usually New Englanders – were committed in principle to racial equality. In the early 1850s, Indiana, Iowa and Illinois passed laws forbidding the immigration of *any* black person, free or slave, largely to placate the racism of white electors, though also to facilitate the operation of the fugitive slave law. By 1860, thirteen states had laws on their statute books barring black freemen from immigrating, while seven required emancipated slaves to leave their territory.

Holy Bible.
Thou shalt not deliver unto the master his servant which has escaped from his master unto thee. He shall dwell with thee. Even among you in that place which he shall choose in one of thy gates where it liketh him best. Thou shalt not oppress him.
Deut XXIII.15.

Effects of the Fugitive-Slave-Law.

Declaration of independence.
We hold that all men are created equal; that they are endowed by their Creator with certain unalienable rights; that among these are life, liberty and the pursuit of happiness.

Figure 16.2 'Effects of the fugitive slave law'. Published by Hoff & Bloede, New York, 1850, lithograph on woven paper, 33.3 x 44.3 cm. Photo: Library of Congress. This is one of many cartoons in the American periodical press depicting the operation of the fugitive slave law.

EXERCISE

What other slavery-related problem did the Constitution leave for a later political generation to settle?

Spend about 10 minutes on this exercise.

SPECIMEN ANSWER

The problem was whether slavery would be allowed in states newly admitted to the Union as the frontier of settlement – and US jurisdiction – moved west.

Slavery and the territorial expansion of the Union

In the republic's early years, the territorial containment of slavery (see Figure 16.3) had not been contentious: with little argument, Congress banned it from the Northwest Territory by the Northwest Ordinance of 1787, which meant that states later carved out of that region were automatically free. The Louisiana Purchase (mentioned in Unit 14) first raised the problem because slavery was already present in this territory, much of which was suitable for plantation agriculture. In 1820, Congress reached a compromise whereby slavery was prohibited north of 36° 30' in the Purchase, though as an exception it was allowed in Missouri north of that line.

What made the issue of slavery's territorial expansion a critical matter for the on-going formation of the USA was the conjunction of three factors in the late 1840s. First, the war against Mexico (1846–7), and the subsequent purchase of Mexican territory, brought further huge areas under US jurisdiction. Second, the war was seen by evangelical northern abolitionists as a conspiracy by the southern 'slave power' to extend its 'peculiar institution' and way of life across the American continent. Southern ideologues openly speculated about creating a 'civilisation' of slave states across the southern rim of North America and the Caribbean, so the notion that the south was destined to be 'an empire for slavery' was not entirely far-fetched.[23] Third, southern planters had a powerful material incentive to reallocate slave labour to newly acquired land in the west, where productivity and the return on capital were higher than in the old south. World demand for cotton was rising by 7 per cent annually. Equally, they had an ideological incentive to assert the legitimacy of slavery against northern demagogues who were mobilising popular politics around the slogans 'Free labor' and 'Free soil'.

The Missouri Compromise of 1820 was shattered when a clique of southern senators insisted on the admission of Kansas to the Union as a slave state as a quid pro quo for admitting Nebraska as a free state. The Kansas–Nebraska Act passed in May 1854 was probably the single most important event pushing the nation towards civil war. 'Free soil' congressmen denounced it as an 'atrocious plot' to convert free territory into 'a dreary region of despotism inhabited by masters and slaves' (McPherson, 1988, pp. 121, 124). It exposed the sectional rift in the American political economy, for northern capitalists had a powerful material interest in slavery's territorial containment: white wage earners would not generally migrate into regions where it was permitted. Slavery impeded the spread of the wage labour 'system' and capitalist enterprise. The issue led to the realignment of American politics and the emergence of the Republican Party, a coalition of the economic and moral interests determined to resist the westward spread of slavery. In reaction to Abraham Lincoln's election in November 1860, seven slave states seceded in January–February and were joined by a further four slave states after the outbreak of war in April.

---

[23] Under President Franklin Pierce (elected in 1852) the USA made serious efforts to acquire the slave colony of Cuba, the world's leading sugar producer.

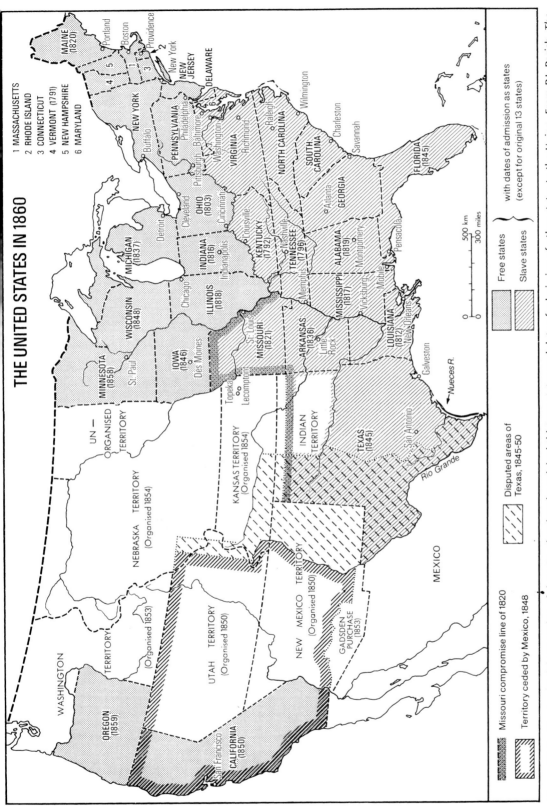

Figure 16.3   The territorial expansion of the USA, showing the original thirteen states and date of admission of other states to the Union. From P.J. Parish, *The American Civil War*, London, Eyre Methuen, 1975.

SLAVE AND SERF PRODUCERS: THE ECONOMICS AND SOCIAL RELATIONS OF BONDED LABOUR

From Tables 16.1 and 16.2, you can form a global sense of the position of serfs in Russian society, and of slaves in the US south, in the half century or so preceding emancipation. Use the information in the tables to write a paragraph comparing the relationship of slaves and serfs to the wider society and the main changes over time revealed by the data. (Note: serfs were conventionally enumerated in terms of taxable male 'souls' and we can assume that there were approximately equal numbers of female serfs at the dates in Table 16.1. Russian census data are deficient and other population estimates differ significantly. The total population was generally reckoned to be 68 million in 1858; in 1795, it was around 39 million.)

Spend about 25 minutes on this exercise.

Table 16.1   Adult male population of Russia, 1795 and 1858 (rounded to the nearest 1,000)

	1795		1858	
	No. of males (k)	% of population	No. of males (k)	% of population
Serfs	9,788	53.9	11,388	39.2
State peasants	6,534	36.0	12,678	43.8
Total peasants	16,322	89.8	24,016	83.0
Noblemen (*pomeshchiki*)	362	2.0	464	1.6
Other	1,484	8.2	4,456	15.4
Total adult male population	18,169		28,935	
Ratio of serfs : noblemen	27.0 : 1		24.4 : 1	
Ratio of peasants : noblemen	45.0 : 1		51.8 : 1	

(Source: Kolchin, 1987, pp. 52–3)

Table 16.2   Population of the US south, 1790 and 1860 (rounded to the nearest 1,000)

	1790		1860	
	No. (k)	% of population	No. (k)	% of population
Slaves	658	33.5	3,951	32.3
Free blacks	32	1.6	254	2.1
Total blacks	690	35.2	4,204	34.4
Individual slave owners			384	
Slave owner family members			1,918	15.7
Other whites			6,119	50.0
Total whites	1,271	64.8	8,037	65.7
Total population	1,961		12,241	
Ratio of slaves : slave owners + family members			2.1 : 1	
Ratio of blacks : whites		0.5 : 1		0.5 : 1

(Source: Kolchin, 1987, pp. 52–3)

We are comparing very different societal entities, since the Russian population was much greater than that of the US south (although the latter's increased far more rapidly). Nearly nine out of ten Russian men were peasants in 1795 and over four out of five were in 1858, so serfs were a substantial segment of an overwhelmingly peasant society. Contrary to popular impressions, they were no longer a majority in the years preceding emancipation; the data suggest a considerable shift from servile status to that of state peasant. Blacks were just over one in three of the total population of the US south at both dates, but nearly all blacks were slaves. The *proportion* of free blacks in the total population rose only slightly over seventy years, which indicates the difficulties in the way of manumission. The near identity of black African descent with bondage obviously had no parallel in Russia. Though only a minority of white southerners owned slaves, slaveholding was more evenly spread among white society than serf holding in Russian society, where noblemen were a tiny fraction of the population. Assuming each slave-owning family was a family of five, then nearly one in four whites belonged to slave-owning families in 1860. Interestingly, these data suggest that the proportions of bonded labourers in the total populations were quite similar on the eve of emancipation: about two-fifths in Russia and one-third in the US south. Absolute numbers of slaves almost kept pace with the growth of total population: very few slaves were imported after 1807, so the black demographic experience must have been similar to the white.

As you will gather from Table 16.3, slaves formed a much greater proportion of the US labour force than they did of the US population because of their exceptional participation rate (about twice that of free labour). Just about all slaves over the age of 10 worked, and there were virtually none of the gender differences evident in the employment of free labour. It has not been possible to find a comparable table for Russian serfs, but it would seem probable that their labour participation rate was higher than that of the state peasants. Before emancipation, there was no large group of *wholly* free workers with whom we can compare the serfs.

Table 16.3   Slaves and the US labour force (rounded to the nearest 1,000)

	US population (k)	Total labour force (k)	Free population (k)	Free labour (k)	Free labour participation rate	Slave population (k) (% of total population)	Slave labour (k) (% of total labour force)	Slave labour participation rate
1820	9,638	3,135	8,100	2,185	27%	1,538 (16%)	950 (30%)	62%
1830	12,866	4,200	10,857	3,020	28%	2,009 (16%)	1,180 (28%)	59%
1840	17,069	5,660	14,581	4,180	29%	2,488 (15%)	1,480 (26%)	59%
1850	23,192	8,250	19,987	6,280	31%	3,205 (14%)	1,970 (24%)	61%
1860	31,443	11,110	27,489	8,770	32%	3,954 (13%)	2,340 (21%)	59%

(Source: US Department of Commerce, *Historical Statistics of the United States: Colonial Times to 1970*. The 'labour force' comprised all those in or seeking gainful employment or self-employment.)

EXERCISE

Now use the data in Tables 16.4 and 16.5 to write a paragraph comparing the distribution of slaves and serfs according to the size of holding in which they lived and worked. (Note: serf holdings were classified according to the number of male souls and we must assume an approximately equal number of female serfs.)

Spend about 20 minutes on this exercise.

Table 16.4   Distribution of American slave owners and slaves by size of holdings, 1860

	No. of slaves owned				
	1–9	10–19	20–49	50–199	>199
% of slave owners	71.9	16.0	9.3	2.6	0.1
% of slaves	25.6	21.6	27.9	22.5	2.4

(Source: Kolchin, 1987, p. 54)

Table 16.4   Distribution of Russian serf owners and serfs by size of holdings, 1858

	No. of male serfs owned			
	1–20	21–100	101–500	>500
% of serf owners	43.6	33.9	18.9	3.6
% of serfs	3.3	15.9	37.2	43.6

(Source: Kolchin, 1987, p. 54)

The data reveal striking differences in the distribution of slaves and serfs. American slavery was dominated by small property owners: the great majority of slave holders had fewer than ten slaves; the great majority of slaves lived in holdings of fewer than fifty. Russian serfdom had a substantial 'tail' of small owners, but they were a smaller proportion of all owners and owned a tiny fraction of the serfs. Four out of five Russian serfs lived in holdings of two hundred or more serfs (assuming equal numbers of females); slaveholdings of that size were very exceptional in the US south.

It is worth adding that elite Russian noblemen each owned tens of thousands of serfs distributed among several estates. The wealthiest nobleman around 1830, Count D. N. Sheremetev, possessed almost 300,000 serfs of both sexes and over 1.9 million acres. Such concentration of wealth and power was inconceivable in the US south, where the typical cotton farmer owned eight slaves. The 1860 census listed only one American slave owner with more than 1,000 slaves, but the 1858 census in Russia counted 3,858 such serf owners. Land ownership in Russia was even more concentrated than the ownership of people. In 1858, over one-half of the 1.9 million square miles of European Russia belonged to private landowners, nearly all of them noblemen (about 1.5 per cent of the population). The rest belonged to the state. Whether or not a southern farmer owned slaves, he almost invariably owned his land. Slave ownership became more concentrated between 1830 and 1860, when the fraction of southern slave-owning households declined from 36 per cent to 25 per cent, but small-scale farmers retained their share of the farmland.

In 1831, a young French lawyer, Alexis de Tocqueville, visited the USA, ostensibly to investigate its penal system, and travelled extensively throughout the country. On his return, he published *Democracy in America*,[24] the most penetrating analysis of democratic society ever penned. The work is full of vivid observations and among the most celebrated is a comparison of Ohio and Kentucky, which have a common border along the Ohio River. Read the passages from Tocqueville reprinted as Anthology Document 4.12, 'Alexis de Tocqueville, *Democracy in America*, 1835–40', and summarise his assessment of the consequences of slavery for the economy and culture of the regions he observed while travelling down the Ohio. Given his assessment, what conclusions would you draw about the economic prospects for

---

[24] The first part appeared in 1835, the second in 1840.

slave-based production around 1830? (To avoid confusion: Tocqueville says Kentucky was founded in 1775 and Ohio in 1787, but they were not admitted as states to the Union until 1792 and 1803, respectively.)

Spend about 40 minutes on this exercise.

SPECIMEN ANSWER

In Tocqueville's view, the economic consequences of slavery in Kentucky had been wholly detrimental by comparison with the free-labour regime in Ohio, which was patently more prosperous and industrially advanced. In Kentucky, slavery had discouraged white immigration and hindered agricultural 'improvement'. Moreover, the aristocratic culture of its slave-owning class appeared hostile to the acquisitive, capitalist values so evident in Ohio. From the final paragraph, one would conclude that the prospects for slave-based production around 1830 were dim: shipping, manufactures, railroads and canals were bound to concentrate in the commercially vibrant north, and attract the more enterprising individuals away from the south.

DISCUSSION

This perfectly reasonable conclusion would have been entirely wrong: slave-based production in the US south was entering a golden age around 1830. It is true that industrialisation (and urbanisation) advanced more rapidly in the north, but the south was not underdeveloped by international standards in 1860. Had the Confederacy seceded peacefully, it would have been an 'advanced' industrial nation state. Among cotton textile producing states, it would have ranked sixth and among pig iron producers, eighth. Only the Union had more railroad mileage per head of population. The south in 1860 was more prosperous than France, Denmark, the German states or, indeed, any European country except England. White southerners were, on average, wealthier than their fellow citizens in the north in 1860 and white per capita income in the south was rising more rapidly.

Why such an intelligent observer as Tocqueville was so mistaken is an interesting question: one reason may be that Kentucky was an economic backwater, but more important – I think – is that, as a student of political economy, Tocqueville was intellectually convinced slavery was an inefficient system of production before he set eyes on actual slaves. (Recall Adam Smith's observations on the supposed economic inefficiency of slave labour that are reproduced in Anthology Document 4.5.) Up to the 1960s, this economic critique of slavery profoundly influenced the historiography of the subject. It led historians to argue – usually from discursive evidence – that the slave-based southern economy was in inexorable decay before the Civil War, with the implication that this great trauma was 'unnecessary'. It took a methodological revolution in economic history to demonstrate the contrary, of which more anon.

Let me add that Tocqueville's readers would also have concluded that the political prospects for the slave-owning class were equally dim, given America's fiercely egalitarian culture. In fact, this class provided the political leadership of an advanced democracy, and not just in the southern states. Southerners dominated the federal government and the Supreme Court up to 1860 and persuaded the legislatures to strengthen slavery's legal bulwarks. Several states passed laws requiring the consent of the legislature to validate the manumission of a slave; still more made it clear they would not tolerate free blacks in their midst. Stricter laws and more severe penalties were also legislated against anyone who helped a slave to run away or who gave absconding slaves asylum. In thirteen states, it became a capital crime for free men to incite slaves to insurrection.

REASON why Southern states seceded

Slavery and the 'cotton kingdom'

Southern prosperity was primarily due to a dominant position in the world market for cotton fibre, the leading industrial crop of its day and the principal employer of slave labour; in 1850, more than half of all southern slaves worked on cotton plantations. Cotton had quite eclipsed the old colonial staples – tobacco, sugar and rice – as an employer of slave labour: their combined slave labour force was one-third the size of cotton's. It is a labour-intensive crop and, before mechanisation, the back-breaking drudgery of planting, hoeing, picking and baling cotton was most efficiently carried out by coordinated labour gangs. Free wage earners could not be persuaded to undertake this work and family farmers without slaves were only marginal producers: they grew less than 10 per cent of output in 1850, though the proportion rose somewhat thereafter. After the outbreak of the Civil War, peasant farmers on the Nile delta were tempted by soaring prices into growing cotton but before then no free producers anywhere consistently matched the productivity of US plantations. This does not mean, however, that the two million slaves on them devoted all their labour time to cotton, nor that their labour was largely unskilled; plantations were usually self-sufficient in food and much of the slaves' time was spent growing their own subsistence. Many slaves were skilled workers and some had managerial functions.

Cotton production in the USA rose from 178,000 bales in 1810 to 4.5 million bales in 1860. It accounted for nearly half US exports between 1840 and 1860, when over three-quarters of the input into the British industry was grown on southern plantations. Planters may have assumed patrician airs but they were hard-headed entrepreneurs, who responded as promptly to price signals as any other capitalists. During the 1850s' cotton boom, as the telegraph delivered exchange prices at the beginning of the planting season, southern farmers shifted about 3 million acres from corn to cotton. Because an acre of cotton requires about 70 per cent more labour than an acre of corn, the demand for gang labour could not be satisfied simply by switching slaves between crops. To supplement their labour gangs, planters paid premium prices for urban slaves: the share of the slave population living in towns declined in the 1850s and the proportion working in the gang system rose.

Over the longer term, the most compelling evidence of alertness to market signals was the westward migration of the cotton frontier. Between 1790 and 1860 some 835,000 slaves were moved, mainly from Maryland, Virginia and the Carolinas, to the western cotton states: Alabama, Mississippi, Louisiana and Texas. Decisions to relocate capital and labour can be closely correlated with booming prices. Some of this movement was due to the internal slave trade, some to the relocation of slave owners (or members of slave-owning families) with their slaves. No scholarly consensus has been reached on what proportion of migrating slaves was sold on, and what proportion accompanied their owners or owners' relatives (Engerman, 2000, p. 339). Both involved forced migration and broke up slave families.

Cotton did not move west because of land shortages in the old south: it makes modest demands on land, but requires a minimum of 200 frost-free days, ample rainfall and does best on alluvial soils. These climatic and ecological factors – assisted by plummeting transport costs – drew capital and labour to the south-western states: their share of the cotton crop rose from 7 per cent to 64 per cent between 1810 and 1840, and to 75 per cent by 1860 (see Figures 16.4 and 16.5). The interregional shift of production factors accounted for nearly one-third of the south's annual growth rate between 1830 and 1860. At the latter date, the average per capita income of free people in the west south central region was substantially higher than in the north-east ($274 a year, as compared with $183). Cotton farmers as a whole became America's wealthiest agrarian entrepreneurs: the average wealth per household of the minority who employed twenty slaves or more in the gang system – and could call themselves 'planters' – was $56,458 in 1860. Throughout the cotton belt, all farmers were worth on average over $13,000, four times as much as the average northern farmer.

Slavery and *Time on the Cross*

More has been written on slavery than on any other topic in American and quite probably world history. Among that vast historiography, no work has been more controversial than *Time on the Cross: The Economics of American Negro Slavery*, published in two volumes in 1974. Few works of economic history have been as widely discussed, or as sharply contested. Yet I suspect quite a few professional historians of slavery have not actually read the work in its entirety: the first volume is perfectly accessible to any student, but the second volume of technical papers – on which the work's many provocative conclusions rest – can be understood only by those competent in the mathematical analysis of quantitative data. The two authors, Robert Fogel[25] and Stan Engerman, were trained as mathematical economists before they came to economic history and throughout their careers have championed cliometrics (from Clio, the muse of history, and metrics, meaning units of measure). Cliometrics's cardinal principle is simple: quantification is the key to explanation in economic history. Most assertions about economic behaviour are implicitly quantitative; cliometricians make these assertions explicit by gathering numerical data (using statistical tests for its reliability) and deploying mathematical formulae to test the relationships between quantified entities. Most of the cliometric revolution has become normal practice in economic history.

Fogel and Engerman conveniently summarised their findings at the beginning of their work – a godsend to students! Those of a 'purely' economic nature, which relate to slavery as a system of production, are now generally accepted. All scholars would agree that:

---

[25] Only the second professional historian ever honoured with a Nobel Prize (for economics).

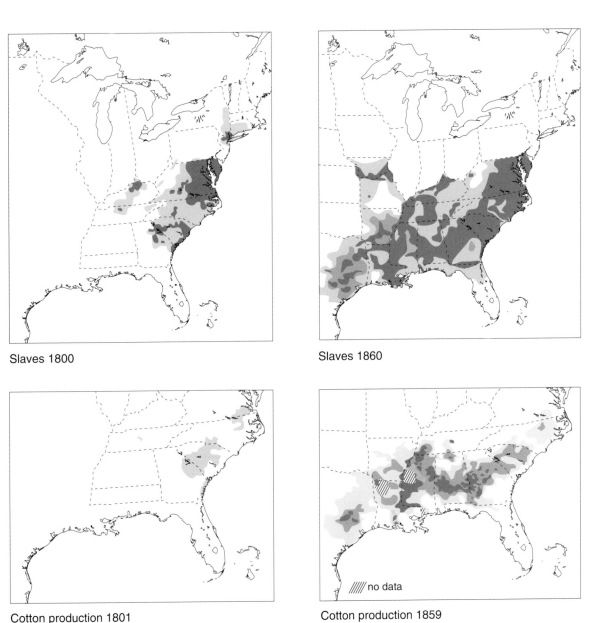

Figure 16.4   The westward movement of cotton and slaves. From Robert William Fogel, *Without Consent or Contract: the Rise and Fall of American Slavery*. Copyright © 1989 by Robert W. Fogel. Used by permission of W.W. Norton & Company Inc.

- Slavery was not a system irrationally kept in operation by plantation owners. The purchase of a slave was a highly profitable investment, yielding rates of return comparable to industrial investments. Fogel and Engerman calculated an average annual rate of return of about 10 per cent on the market price of slaves, which was about the same average rate of return earned by nine of the most successful New England textile firms between 1844 and 1853 and more than the average return of twelve southern railroads in the 1850s.

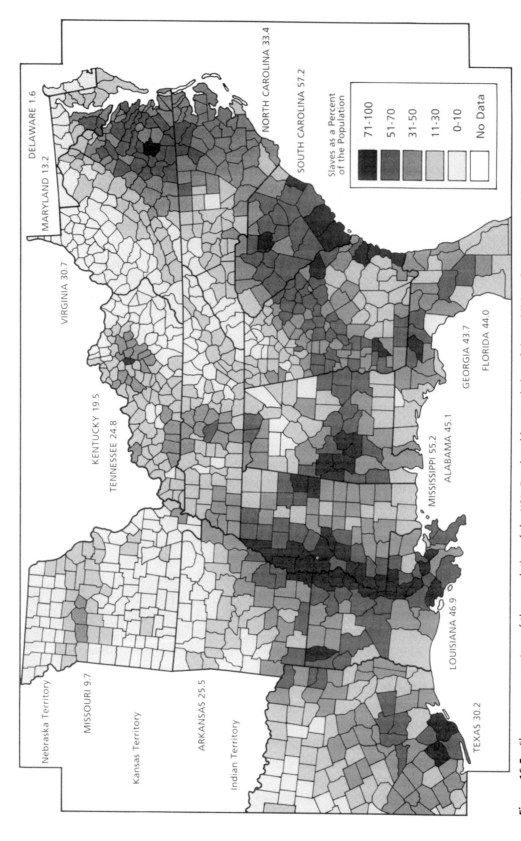

Figure 16.5   Slaves as a percentage of the population of the USA. Reprinted by permission of the publisher from Peter Kolchin, *Unfree Labor: American Slavery and Russian Serfdom*, Cambridge, Mass. and London: Belknap Press of Harvard University Press, © 1987 by the President and fellows of Harvard College

- The system was not economically moribund in 1860. Economic forces alone would not have brought it to an end. There are no grounds for asserting that slavery was incompatible with the shifting labour requirements of capitalist society. The rental market for slave labour in southern cities – where slaves were about a third of skilled artisans – demonstrates the system's adaptability to social modernisation.
- Slaveholders anticipated an era of unprecedented prosperity on the eve of the Civil War. Slave prices doubled between the mid-1840s and 1860, which reflected the high level of immediate profits and the bounding optimism of slave owners regarding future prospects. Between 1857 and 1860, cotton output doubled as demand soared in New England and 'old' England.
- Slave agriculture was not inefficient compared with free agriculture. Economies of scale, effective management and more intensive utilisation of labour and capital made slave agriculture about a third more efficient than northern family farming. Plantation labour gangs of twenty or more worked so intensively that they produced as much output in roughly 35 minutes as did free farmers in an hour.
- Far from stagnating, the ante-bellum southern economy grew rapidly. White per capita income in the south increased more quickly than in the rest of the nation between 1840 and 1860 (Fogel and Engerman, 1974, pp. 5–6, *passim*).

Time on the Cross and the slave family

However, Fogel and Engerman claimed to have demonstrated far more than the viability of a system of production. Behind the hard-nosed econometric calculations were challenging claims about the social psychology of slavery and the slave family. Slaveholders, they asserted, did not rely principally on the whip to raise labour output, but offered their slaves material incentives (better food, time off, passes to see relatives and friends on other plantations). As a consequence, the slaves' material condition compared favourably with industrial workers. Like all rural populations, they were spared the devastating infant mortality of nineteenth-century cities: a child born into US slavery in 1850 had a better expectation of life than a child born in New York or Manchester in 1850. Slaves for their part were neither the plodding 'Sambos' of racist stereotype nor the everyday resistance fighters of left-wing mythology: they were skilled, hard-working and efficient workers who had imbibed the Protestant work ethic and Victorian family values. Slaves were not promiscuous: they formed stable family units, which – according to Fogel and Engerman – their masters were reluctant to disrupt by separating husbands and wives and parents and children.

These claims were – and remain – fiercely contested: Herbert Gutman, an authority on the black family, considered Fogel's and Engerman's 'generalizations about the slave family and slave sexual behaviour ... so lacking in documentation that they do not deserve serious discussion' (Gutman, 1975, p. 90). He then subjected these generalisations to minute scrutiny and found them conceptually flawed and evidentially ill-founded. Gutman was especially scathing of their use of the invoices of slave sales in New Orleans – the largest market in the interregional slave trade – to conclude that only a tiny fraction of slave marriages were destroyed by enforced westward migration and that children were very rarely sold separately from their parents. (Gutman, 1975, devoted nearly eighty closely argued pages to the analysis of the slave family, slave sexual behaviour and slave sales in *Time on the Cross*.)

The ramifications of this debate cannot be pursued here. Suffice to say that, while cliometricians may quantify the frequency of family break up, they cannot measure its pain. Slave autobiographies and oral life histories gathered from elderly ex-slaves by teams of researchers in 1920s and 1930s testify to the chronic threat to family life posed by forced separation. The words of an old Virginia black woman, recorded three-quarters of a century after the end of slavery, remain devastatingly eloquent:

> No white ever been in my house. Don't 'low it. Dey sole my sister Kate. I saw it wid dese here eyes. Sole her in 1860, and I ain't seed nor heard of her since. Folks say white folks is all right dese days. Maybe dey is, maybe dey isn't. But I can't stand to see 'em. Not on my place.
>
> (Quoted in Kolchin, 1987, p. 116)

Serf labour and the Russian economy

There was a striking contrast between the bullish optimism of American slaveholders in the 1850s and the pessimism of Russian serf owners. The former expected their social order to endure and foresaw an era of prosperity; the latter sensed that emancipation was imminent and the more enlightened welcomed the prospect. 'Slavery', writes Kolchin, 'flourished as never before, [but] Russian serfdom constituted a bankrupt system widely recognised as on its last legs' (Kolchin, 1987, p. 362). Statistical evidence for this bankruptcy can be found in the landlords' practice of mortgaging serfs as collateral for loans taken out with special government credit bureaux. In 1820, 20 per cent of all serfs were mortgaged against loans totalling 110 million roubles; by 1859, two-thirds of all serfs were mortgaged and the loan total had risen to 425 million roubles (Blum, 1961, p. 380). Fortunately, the state was an indulgent creditor, and rarely foreclosed on indebted landowners. The thousands who owned fewer than twenty male serfs lived in extremely straitened circumstances; those who resided on their estates were often indistinguishable from peasants. By American standards, they had ample bonded labour at their command, so why were they such an economically depressed class?

Much of the answer lies in the socio-cultural characteristics of the *pomeshchiki* who, you will recall, were originally assigned land and serfs in exchange for serving the state. Even after obligatory service ended, they had remained tribute takers, not agrarian capitalists. Most were absentee landlords who delegated the running of their estates to serf stewards, and used agrarian income to support an urban lifestyle; outside the fertile black earth belt, few were directly involved in production. Where they did farm their demesne, the techniques employed were often no better than the serfs'.

The novelist Ivan Goncharov painted a hilarious but deeply critical portrait of the typical *pomeshchik* in *Oblomov*, first published in 1859 (Goncharov, 1963 [1859]). Its anti-hero, Ilya Ilych Oblomov, is the scion of a once-wealthy and illustrious family who had inherited 350 serfs in one of the distant provinces bordering on Asia. When the novel opens we find that Oblomov has been living in a cramped two-room flat in St Petersburg with a single elderly retainer. He had come to the capital twelve years before in search of the official position to which his social and bureaucratic rank[26] entitled him, while living – at first comfortably, but latterly in reduced circumstances – on the income from his estates. Over the years, indolence had become habitual: in the opening chapters, Oblomov can scarcely rise from bed and receives visitors in his shabby dressing gown. He has mislaid a letter from his serf steward but when eventually located in the bed clothes, it makes distressing reading:

> Dear Sir, Your Honor, our father and benefactor, Ilya Ilych ... I wish to inform your noble grace that on your ancestral estate, dear benefactor, all is well. No rain for five weeks. The good Lord, it seems, must be angry with us that He sends no rain. The old folks cannot recall such a drought ever. The spring crops were scorched as in a frying pan. Some of the winter crops were ruined by worms and some by early frosts. I had it ploughed under for a spring crop, but there's no telling if anything will come up. Let's hope the merciful Lord will have mercy on your noble grace; as for ourselves, we don't mind if we perish. And on St John's Eve three more peasants ran away: Laptev and Balochov, and what's more, Vaska, the blacksmith's son, left too. I sent the women after their husbands, but they never came back, and it is said they are living at Cholki ... .I appealed to the police inspector [about the runaways] and he said: 'Send in a statement and measures will be taken to return their peasants to their place of domicile.' That's all he said, so I went down on my knees before him with tears in my eyes, but he yelled with all his might: 'Get out! Get out! I've told you it would be done. Send in the statement.' But I did not send it in. There is no one here I can hire. They have all gone to the Volga to work on the barges. We will have no linen at the fair this year. I locked up the drying and bleaching sheds and set Sychuga to watch over them day and night. He is a sober man, and to make sure he does not filch my master's goods I watch over him day and night. The others drink heavily and only want

---

[26] By the early nineteenth century, the service class was graded according to rank in the state bureaucracy which a *pomeshchik* of a particular grade could enter. Oblomov had the rank of collegiate secretary – although he never actually secured a job of that rank.

to pay quitrent. The taxes are in arrears. This year we will send less
income, our father and benefactor, about two thousand less than we
sent last year, unless the drought ruins us completely, otherwise we
will send what we have stated to your grace ... Your steward and most
humble serf ... .signed by his own hand.

(Goncharov, 1963 [1859], p. 54)

Of course, the steward is remorselessly fleecing the master, but Oblomov is too
lazy to write to the governor of his province to complain. He passes the novel
in resigned idleness.

How useful is a literary source such as this for historians? Goncharov came
from a noble family whose estates had dwindled through mismanagement and
there are elements of self-portrait in his anti-hero. It is a 'realist' novel in that
its author strove for social and psychological verisimilitude, but like any good
novelist he used his creative imagination to re-assemble elements of the social
world into a narrative fiction. Perhaps the accuracy of the literary depiction is
less important than the fact that educated Russians immediately seized on
Oblomov as a brilliant diagnosis of the social parasitism inherent in a serf-
owning society. 'Oblomovism' entered the language as a synonym for genteel
fecklessness.

There is, in fact, no evidence of a *general* decline in serf owners' incomes in
the decades preceding serf emancipation, although numerous small proprietors
were in severe difficulties. Two quite different trends indicated that the more
enterprising *pomeshchiki* were adapting serfdom to the requirements of
extended market production. Some were imposing harsher labour obligations
(*barshchina*) and converting more of their land to demesne or fields on which
they owned the crop. To compensate for the loss of their strips, the serfs would
be allocated a food ration. But other large landowners were increasing their
own money incomes by converting their serfs' obligations from labour to what
was in effect rent (*obrok* paid in cash). They were encouraged to do this by
growth of the exchange economy, which made it easier for serfs to accumulate
cash. Living off rising rents was less demanding of entrepreneurial skill and
capital than the commercial exploitation of peasant labour. The contrast with
American slave owners, who mostly lived on their farms and directly managed
their businesses, is instructive. Nothing resembling the gang labour system was
imposed on serfs, who lived in autonomous, self-governing village
communities and were notoriously resistant to changes in their agricultural
routine.

The contrast between tribute-taking serf owners and slave-owning agrarian
capitalists should not be overdrawn. Russia had its own 'deep south' in the
provinces of New Russia (bordering the Black Sea) and in Little Russia and
the southwest region, immediately to the north (see Figure 16.1) In the first
half of the nineteenth century, commercial farming boomed in Russia's 'deep
south', where 97 per cent and more of male serfs had to perform *barshchina*.
Labour demands became more onerous as landowners sought to capture export
markets in western Europe. Regional economic specialisation allowed for more

intensive agriculture: shoes, clothes and basic implements were increasingly produced by industries located around Moscow and St Petersburg, rather than within the village, which meant serfs devoted all their labour to the fields. But even the level of coerced labour prevailing in the 'deep south' did not meet all the landlords' labour requirements; each year they hired thousands of serfs and state peasants who came from the central provinces in search of seasonal employment. By 1850, an estimated 300,000 migratory workers were employed each season. Diversification into new crops, especially sugar beet, and agro-industries (sugar refining and distilling) created new demands for serf labour. By 1861, there were 448 sugar beet mills in southern Russia, nearly all owned and operated by landlords employing their own serfs. Some 40,000 to 50,000 serfs fulfilled their *barshchina* obligations in the sugar mills, alongside about 20,000 hired labourers. A further 90,000 serfs were employed in the southern distilleries at this time, which were mostly established by landowners using their own bonded labour.

THE IDEOLOGIES OF BONDED LABOUR

On 4 March 1858, Senator James Hammond of South Carolina made a celebrated speech to the Senate. In the previous year, a wave of bankruptcies had ripped through the northern economy and only a great increase in raw cotton exports had saved northern capitalism from financial collapse. This, claimed Hammond, was testimony to the superiority of slavery over so-called free labour:

> In all social systems there must be a class to do the menial duties, to perform the drudgery of life. That is a class requiring but a low order of intellect and but little skill. Its requisites are vigor, docility, and fidelity. Such a class you must have, or you would not have that other class which leads progress, civilization, and refinement. It constitutes the very mud-sill of society and of political government; and you might as well attempt to build a house in the air, as to build the one or the other except on this mud sill ... [Addressing the northern senators, Hammond went on:] Your hireling class of manual laborers and 'operatives', as you call them, are essentially slaves. The difference between us is, that our slaves are hired for life and well compensated ... yours are hired by the day, not cared for, and scantily compensated.
> (Quoted in Kolchin, 1987, pp. 172–3, McPherson, 1988, p. 196)

Hammond articulated key themes in an ideology of slavery which took on a hegemonic function in ante-bellum society. By this I mean that the majority of whites who did not own slaves were increasingly persuaded that slavery was in their interests and essential for the south's way of life, culture and values. The defence of slavery persuaded an otherwise truculent electorate of independent small farmers to defer to the political and social leadership of the planter class. A moral consensus formed around the 'peculiar institution', and the right to maintain it became something for which hundreds of thousands willingly fought and died.

EXERCISE

How, in social terms, would you describe the ethic behind Hammond's defence of slavery? Why was it so discordant with the basic principles of American political life?

Spend about 10 minutes on this exercise.

SPECIMEN ANSWER

The term I would choose is 'aristocratic'. It could also be described by an expression such as 'the ethic of a caste society'. Hammond assumed an inevitable division between a class of helots and an aristocratic elite which 'leads progress, civilization and refinement'. This was discordant with equality of legal and social status which is a basic principle of American political life, as illustrated by the fact that the Constitution prohibits titles of nobility.

DISCUSSION

One of the paradoxes to emerge from comparing the ideologies of slavery and serfdom is that the southern planter elite (and the newspapermen and clergy who acted as its spokesmen) saw itself as a 'true' aristocracy, while the Russian nobility had little of an aristocracy's collective self-confidence. The clue to unravelling this paradox lies in the political impotence of the *pomeshchiki* and their subservience to the state. Their lands and serfs had historically been assigned to them by the autocracy, on whom they normally depended for state employment; they were resigned to the fact that the autocracy could revoke these privileges as it pleased. The southern planter class had created both a weak state and an exceptionally secure legal environment for private property, including slaves. By a strategy of skilful populism – 'licking the arses of the voters' as one slave owner put it – they had taken a grip on the political leadership of southern society. They needed the state only to secure a favourable tariff regime, sound money and an effective fugitive slave law. The planter class could openly discuss extreme political steps (secession, civil war) which were simply beyond the political imagination of Russian landowners.

[handwritten margin note: little influence on state policy]

[handwritten margin note: 'slave-owning' states elected senators to Congress, part of the legislature.]

The paternalism that was such a pronounced feature of the ideology of southern slavery was consistent with this aristocratic ethic. Again, the contrast with the attitudes of Russian serf owners is striking. Particularly in the pre-war decades, a host of southern publicists trumpeted the humane reciprocity of slavery: the masters cared for the slaves' physical and spiritual welfare and the slaves were docilely contented with their fate. It became a cliché to contrast the bondman's comfortable lot with the misery of 'wage slavery', while depicting the south as a haven of tradition and the north as an anarchic cesspit. One polemicist wrote in 1854: 'Let the North enjoy their hireling labor with all its ... pauperism, rowdyism, mobism and anti-rentism ... We do not want it. We are satisfied with our slave labor ... We like old things – old wine, old books, old friends, old and fixed relations between employer and employer' (quoted in McPherson, 1988, p. 99). Of course, this rationalisation for bondage was self-serving and – to us – deeply repugnant, but in a grossly distorted way it refracted certain historical realities. Slave owners normally resided on the same estate or farm as their slaves and knew them by name. When they left written instructions to farm managers, these often emphasised ensuring an adequate diet, not overworking pregnant women and the sick, and moderation in corporal punishment. Serf owners were usually absentees and the serf commune was a more distant community, and in some ways more alien than the slave quarters were to the master. In their instructions to estate managers, serf owners were rarely concerned with the physical and moral welfare of their serfs; these were matters which they left to the *mir* or peasant commune (the word also means 'world'). They worried, instead, about securing *obrok* payments and labour dues and ensuring taxes were paid. The typical Russian estate was said to be 'seigniorial property, but peasant domain'; the proprietor's impact on its pattern of life and work was negligible. *see: Chekhov's "The Cherry Orchard"*

Two interrelated themes in the ideology of slavery were the Biblical justification of bondage and the claim that ethnic descent – so-called race – fitted some for slavery. Southern pastors were still asserting in the 1850s that 'the doom of Ham has been branded on the form and features of his African descendants'. Somewhat incongruously, this ancient prejudice was being fortified by quasi-scientific accounts of ethnic difference which claimed to demonstrate the innate inferiority of blacks. There were muted analogues in the ideology of serfdom: noble authors sometimes construed the serfs as a race apart, separated not only by manners and culture but also by breeding from polite society. But given the common ethnicity of all Russians, and the increasing awareness of Slav identity in literate circles, this theme had a limited currency.

Interestingly, the boldest and most consistent of American pro-slavery advocates in 1840s and 1850s were themselves increasingly downplaying race as a justification for slavery. They emphasised the superiority of a bondage-based social system over free wage labour, which they painted as a transient and unstable experiment in a few corners of the western world.

TWO EMANCIPATIONS COMPARED

Within a relatively short space of time, the leaders of two of the most powerful states in the Christian world issued emancipation proclamations. In February 1861, Tsar Alexander II decreed: 'The serfdom of the peasants who live on seigniorial property and of household serfs is abolished forever ...'. *"Emancipation Proclamation"* Henceforth, they were 'free, rural inhabitants'. On 22 September 1862, President Abraham Lincoln proclaimed that slaves in the rebellious Confederate states would, from 1 January 1863, be 'thenceforward and forever free'. *"freeing 4 million slaves"* The circumstances of these two proclamations could scarcely have been more different. Lincoln's was a wartime measure, issued after it had become clear that the Civil War would be more protracted and bloodier than expected. Had the Union achieved a quick victory over the Confederacy, then slave emancipation would not have resulted. In July 1861, Lincoln had reaffirmed in a message to Congress that he had 'no purpose, directly or indirectly, to interfere with slavery in the States where it exists' (McPherson, 1988, p. 312). The Constitution did not empower the president to confiscate the property of US citizens, which is why slaves in the 'border states' that had remained loyal to the Union were excluded from the proclamation.[27] However, as commander-in-chief, Lincoln was empowered to seize *enemy* property. Emancipation was an instrument of economic warfare, intended to deny the Confederacy essential labour. But it also changed the character of the war by openly inciting the

---

[27] The 'border states' were Missouri, Kentucky, Maryland and Delaware, which permitted slave owning but did not secede on the outbreak of war on 12 April 1861.

slaves to flee, by sanctioning the enlistment of black soldiers and sailors in Union forces, and by equating Union victory with the destruction of the south's 'peculiar institution'. From 1 January, the Union armies would be armies of liberation.

Whereas Lincoln's proclamation was extemporised, the tsarist edict had been long prepared. Serfdom was a discredited institution in Russia from the 1840s, if not earlier. Alexander's father, Nicholas I, had described it as 'an evil, palpable and obvious for all' in an address to his council of state in March 1842, and had anticipated 'a gradual transition to a different order ...' (Seton-Watson, 1967, p. 227). However, the 1848 revolutions – which led to a spate of serf emancipations elsewhere in central and eastern Europe – prompted a stifling reaction in Russia. All discussion of reform was censored in the years preceding Nicholas's death in 1855. The autocracy was shaken out of its stasis by defeat in the Crimean War (1854–6) which exposed Russia's economic, technological and social backwardness by comparison with the victorious liberal powers, France and Britain. Widespread rural unrest may have persuaded Alexander of the need to forestall a serf rebellion. On 30 March 1856, he told a meeting of the nobility of Moscow: 'It is better to abolish serfdom from above than to wait until the serfs begin to liberate themselves from below' (Seton-Watson, 1967, p. 355). Shortly thereafter, he appointed a committee of senior officials to draw up the basic principles of an emancipation edict. It quickly established that the landowners were not to be compensated for the loss of the person of the serf. The thorny questions were whether the emancipated serfs would own the land they used for their own subsistence and how much the landowners would be compensated for relinquishing their ownership over part of their land. Furthermore, serfdom was a system of rural government, as well as agrarian production, and some substitute had to be found for the judicial authority the landowners exercised over their serfs. Under the emancipation edict, the peasants were broadly entitled to the land they used, but full ownership was to come through paying annual 'redemption dues'. Much of the landowners' administrative power was transferred to the village assembly or *obshchina*, which assumed collective responsibility for paying taxes and the redemption dues.

Paradoxically, Europe's most autocratic and reactionary state abolished personal bondage some years before the great American democracy amended its Constitution to outlaw slavery. Lincoln was re-elected on an abolition platform in November 1864, when the Confederacy's ultimate defeat was clearly inevitable (though its main army did not surrender until 9 April 1865.) The 13th amendment abolishing slavery was passed by the necessary two-thirds majority in the House on 31 January, and subsequently ratified by three-quarters of *all* states (including those in the Confederacy.) The slave owners were not compensated for the loss of their property, but no general provision was made either to ensure that emancipated slaves could exercise citizenship rights or to give them title to land. Under the Federal Constitution, voting eligibility was decided by the state legislatures. In his final public speech, Lincoln voiced his wish that 'reconstructed' states occupied by Union armies would enfranchise literate negroes and black veterans. One listener, John Wilkes Booth, snarled to a companion: 'That means nigger citizenship. Now, by God, I'll put him through. That is the last speech he will ever make' (McPherson, 1988, p. 852). Lincoln was assassinated on Good Friday. As it happened, Alexander II – the tsar liberator – was also assassinated, on 1 March 1881, by political terrorists endeavouring to liberate the Russian masses.

Both emancipations left massive social problems unsolved; nevertheless, both were irreversible steps towards a modernity in which the idea of personal bondage was unthinkable.

CONCLUSION

This unit should have helped you understand how slavery and a variant of serfdom close to slavery coexisted with vastly different political institutions and cultures in the Christian world. It should have enlightened you – if only a little – as to why they persisted so long, and what brought them to end.

EXERCISE

As a way of reprising the block as a whole, consider this passage from the great nineteenth-century liberal philosopher John Stuart Mill, writing soon after emancipation. How, according to Mill, had slavery been justified in western culture since Antiquity and in his own lifetime? In attacking the rationale for slavery, Mill was also attacking the rationale for another form of servitude; what was it? Does this passage give you a particular insight into why the term 'slavery' resonates so powerfully in our culture?

> [W]as there ever any domination which did not appear natural to those who possessed it? There was a time when the division of mankind into two classes, a small one of masters and a numerous one of slaves, appeared even to the most cultivated minds, to be a natural, and the only natural condition of the human race. No less an intellect, and one which contributed no less to the progress of human thought, than Aristotle, held this opinion without doubt or misgiving; and rested it on the same premises on which the assertion in regard to the dominion of men over women is usually based, namely that there are different natures among mankind, free natures and slave natures; that the Greeks were of a free nature, the barbarian races of Thracians and Asiatics of a slave nature. But why need I go back to Aristotle? Did not the slave owners of the Southern United States maintain the same doctrine, with all the fanaticism with which men cling to their theories that justify their passions and legitimate their personal interests? Did they not call heaven and earth to witness that the dominion of the white man over the black is natural, that the black race is by nature incapable of freedom, and marked out for slavery?
>
> (Mill, 1975 [1869], p.440)

Spend about 15 minutes on this exercise.

SPECIMEN ANSWER

Slavery had been justified since Antiquity on the grounds that there were innate natural differences between masters and slaves. In Mill's day, the subjection of women to men was justified in identical terms; he was using the speciousness of pro-slavery arguments to expose the equally dubious arguments for the political and legal subordination of women to men. The passage gives us an insight into the cultural resonance of 'slavery' because it so clearly relates the historical phenomenon of slavery to racism: the enslavement of black people was tolerable because they were considered natural inferiors, a prejudice that persisted long after the institution was outlawed. Mill's eloquent scorn for pro-slavery arguments testifies to the resonance of 'slavery' in his day, when the battle cry of freedom was still echoing across the Atlantic.

REFERENCES

Blum, J. (1961) *Lord and Peasant in Russia: From the Ninth to the Nineteenth Century*, Princeton, Princeton University Press.

Blum, J. (1978) *The End of the Old Order in Rural Europe*, Princeton, Princeton University Press.

Engerman, S.L. (2000) 'Slavery and its consequences for the south in the nineteenth century', in Engerman, S.L. and Gallman, R.E. (eds), *The Cambridge Economic History of the United States*; vol. 2 *The Long Nineteenth Century*, Cambridge, Cambridge University Press.

Field, D. (1976) *The End of Serfdom: Nobility and Bureaucracy in Russia 1855–1861*, Cambridge, Mass., Harvard University Press.

Fogel, R.W. and Engerman, S.L. (1974) *Time on the Cross: The Economics of American Negro Slavery*, 2 vols, New York, Little, Brown.

Fogel, R.W. (1989) *Without Consent or Contract: The Rise and Fall of American Slavery*, New York, Norton.

Goncharov, I. (1963 [1859]) *Oblomov*, trans. A. Dunnigan, New York, Signet Classics.

Gutman, H.G. (1975) *Slavery and the Numbers Game: A Critique of Time on the Cross*, Chicago, University of Illinois Press.

Kolchin, P. (1987) *Unfree Labor: American Slavery and Russian Serfdom*, Cambridge, Mass., Harvard University Press.

McPherson, J. (1988) *Battle Cry of Freedom: The Civil War Era*, Oxford, Oxford University Press.

Mill, J.S. (1975 [1869]) 'The subjection of women', in *Three Essays* (with an introduction by R. Wollheim), Oxford, Oxford University Press.

Pipes, R. (1974) *Russia under the Old Regime*, London, Weidenfeld & Nicolson.

Radishchev, A. (1958 [1790]) *Journey from St Petersburg to Moscow*, Cambridge, Mass., Harvard University Press.

Seton-Watson, H. (1967) *The Russian Empire 1801–1917*, Oxford, Oxford University Press.

Smith, A. (1910 [1776]) *The Wealth of Nations*, London, Everyman.

FURTHER READING

Unit 13

Blackburn, R. (1997) *The Making of New World Slavery: From the Baroque to the Modern 1492–1800*, New York, Verso, 1997.

Eltis, D. (1987) *Economic Growth and the Ending of the Atlantic Slave Trade*, Oxford, Oxford University Press.

Sheridan, R.B. (1998) 'The formation of Caribbean plantation society, 1698–1748' in Marshall, P.J. (ed.) *The Oxford History of the British Empire: the Eighteenth Century*, Oxford, Oxford University Press, 1998.

Unit 14

Blackburn, R. (1997) *The Making of New World Slavery: From the Baroque to the Modern, 1492–1800*, New York, Verso.

Eltis, D. (2000) *The Rise of African Slavery in the Americas*, Cambridge, Cambridge University Press.

McKendrick, N., Brewer, J. and Plumb, J.H. (1983) *The Birth of a Consumer Society: The Commercialization of Eighteenth-century England*, London, Europa.

Morgan, K. (2000) *Slavery, Atlantic Trade and the British Economy, 1660–1800*, Cambridge, Cambridge University Press.

Unit 15

Butler, K.M. (1995) *The Economics of Emancipation: Jamaica and Barbados, 1823–1843*, Chapel Hill, University of North Carolina Press.

Davis, D.B. (1970) *The Problem of Slavery in Western Culture*, Harmondsworth, Penguin.

Davis, D.B. (1975) *The Problem of Slavery in the Age of Revolution 1776–1823*, Ithaca, Cornell University Press.

Drescher, S. (1977) *Econocide: British Slavery in the Era of Emancipation*, Pittsburgh, University of Pittsburgh Press.

Fogel, R.W. (1989) *Without Consent or Contract: The Rise and Fall of American Slavery*, New York, Norton.

Midgley, C. (1992) *Women Against Slavery: the British Campaigns, 1780–1870*, London, Routledge.

Turner, M. (1982) *Slaves and Missions: The Disintegration of Jamaican Slave Society, 1787–1834*, Chicago, University of Illinois Press.

Walvin, J. (1992) *Black Ivory: A History of British Slavery*, London, HarperCollins.

Walvin, J. (ed.) (1982) *Slavery and British Society, 1776–1846*, Basingstoke, Macmillan.

Unit 16

Gutman, H.G. (1976) *The Black Family in Slavery and Freedom 1750–1925*, Oxford, Blackwell.

GLOSSARY

Absolutism
early modern theory of government claiming that monarchs were, by divine right, entitled to rule absolutely (i.e. without reference to parliament or the assembled estates of the realm)

Aggregate demand
the total demand for goods and services, including demand arising from export markets and investment (the term was given wider currency in economic thinking by J.M. Keynes)

Autarky/autarkic
economic self-sufficiency

Autocracy
absolute rule by a single person

Barshchina (Russ.)
labour obligations of serfs

Calculative rationality
the rationality social actors demonstrate when they try to calculate the consequences of their actions in terms of profit and loss; the social theorist, Max Weber, considered that double-entry book keeping epitomised calculative rationality

Capital accumulation
investment in capital goods; the process by which capitalists increase their stock of machines etc. which raise the productivity of labour and so increase output

Chartered company/corporation
in the early modern period, a company of merchants granted exclusive commercial rights by royal charter

Chattel slavery
the ownership of one person by another

Cliometrics
historical sub-discipline emphasising measurement and the application of economic theory to problems in economic history

Commodity production
production of any goods for the market or monetary exchange

Commodity structure (of exports, imports etc)

the distribution of a given quantity of commodities amongst different types of commodities (principally raw materials, foodstuffs, manufactures)

Counter factuality

a methodological device by which historians gauge the significance of an historical fact or process by comparing it with a plausible 'counter fact'; the classic instance of counter factual enquiry is Robert Fogel's attempt to measure the measure the significance of railroads for economic growth in the nineteenth-century US economy by comparing the actual economy c.1890 with a counter factual model in which the US economy developed without railroads and the investment allocated to railroads was re-allocated to canals, road improvements etc

Creole

from the Spanish, criollo, which originally meant an American-born Hispanic of pure European descent; the term creole came to be applied to anyone (black, white or of mixed decent) born in the West Indies

Discursive evidence

evidence which 'talks about' or describes that to which it refers

Econometric

refers to the measurement of economic quantities; econometric history is essentially quantitative

Evangelical

originally applied to Christians who believed in the doctrine of salvation by faith alone

Feudal mode of production/capitalist mode of production

the concept of 'mode of production' is central to Marx's theory of history although nowhere clearly explicated in his writings. It refers essentially to the way in which the dominant class extracts an economic surplus from the great mass of producers. In the feudal mode of production, most worked on the land and the surplus was extracted principally by coercion: peasants were compelled to spend part of their working week tilling the lords' fields. In the capitalist mode of production, the surplus is generated by free wage labour: workers voluntarily contract with their employers to exchange their labour for money

Gross domestic product (GDP)/ gross national product (GNP

GDP = the total market value of goods and services produced within a designated economy in a specified time (usually a year); GNP = the total market value of the goods and services produced by a country's nationals in a specified time; the difference between the two is that GNP includes the product of investments abroad which eventually flows back to the domestic economy; GDP is theoretically equal to gross domestic income and GNP to gross national income; i.e. the income from the goods and services marketed in a specified time

Gross industrial product (GIP)

the total market value of the output of manufacturing

Hegemony/hegemonic

in the original Greek, hegemony simply meant the leadership of one state within a confederation. The term was popularised in 'western' neo-Marxism in the 1960s and 1970s because of the great interest in the posthumously published writings of the Italian communist leader, Antonio Gramsci (d.1939); for Gramsci, 'hegemony' referred to process by which the ruling class actively mobilises the consent of the subordinate classes by offering them moral leadership

Kholopy (Russ.)

slaves

L'exclusif (French)

term used for the system of mercantilist regulation in C17[th] and C18th France; mostly devised by Louis XIV's minister, Colbert

Labour productivity

refers to the rate of output of a given unit of labour in a specified time. (Note it is quite possible for labour productivity to rise, although total production falls: for example, take a factory where 100 workers produce 1000 cars week; if 50 workers are laid off, and the factory then produces 750 cars a week, then labour productivity or output per worker will have risen, though production has fallen)

Manorial economy

refers to a system of production based predominantly on the manor or locality: most goods were locally produced and consumed; there was little production for distant markets; much economic activity was not monetised

Manumission

legal process by which a slave was granted his or her freedom

Maroons

from the Spanish, cimarron (wild); applied to runaway slaves, especially those who had formed autonomous communities beyond the reach of planter power

Mercantilism

historians' term for the regulatory economic systems introduced by early modern states to ensure a positive balance of payments; usually involved a national monopoly on colonial trade and tariff discrimination against foreign vessels, as well as the absolute ban on importing certain manufactures to protect domestic producers; in Adam Smith's *The Wealth of Nations* mercantilism – a term he did not use – is referred to as 'the mercantile system of political economy'

Mir (Russ.)

peasant commune

'Malthusian' crisis

from T.R.Malthus (d.1835), the pioneer demographer; refers to the social crisis which arises when population growth outstrips the means of subsistence and hunger-related mortality suddenly increases; the best known example in the history of the British Isles is the Irish famine of 1845-7

Modernity

generally refers to a *concatenation* or linked series of intellectual, economic, technological and political processes, which originated in western Europe in the C17th and reshaped global society in subsequent centuries. At the core of this concatenation were the rise of nomological science (i.e. science that resulted in predictive laws); the overseas expansion of European capitalism and the emergence of an intercontinental division of labour; the origins of a new political form, the national state; and exceptional mechanical creativity. Intellectually, modernity was associated with the radical scepticism of the individual sovereign mind (the Cartesian ego) and, therefore, the subversion of dogma and tradition. Economically, modernity was coterminous with the global extension of the market (including the market in labour). Politically, modernity was expressed in the secularisation of legitimate power and the use of natural law to develop theories of human rights. The technological quintessence of early modernity was the watch, which allowed the individual to measure time wherever he or she might be. The homogenisation of 'human' time and space – which has led global society to orient itself to the same temporal and spatial measure – is one of modernity's most remarked upon cultural consequences. It is well known that western Europe was indebted to other cultures (China, Islam, and indirectly Hindu India) for crucial components of modernity (printing, gun-powder, the mathematical concept of zero, anatomical knowledge – the list of borrowings is extensive) but the *concatenation* I have outlined was unique to western Europe. The archaeology of modernity would reveal 'layers' of apparently modern consciousness sedimented in the Reformation and the Italian Renaissance, but the concatenation to which I refer was not effected until the C17th.

Muzhiki (Russ.)

lit. 'little men', peasants, serfs

Obrok (Russ.)

quitrent paid by peasants in cash or kind

Patrimonial state

a state in which the land and people are the ruler's patrimony or property inherited from his (or, more rarely, her) father, with the implication that the ruler has a duty of care so that patrimony can be passed on to his (or her) son. (Many states classed as patrimonial have excluded female succession.)

Political economy

has two basic meanings: the first is what we now call 'development economics', the branch of economic science which seeks to explain how predominantly agrarian formations are transformed into industrialised (and more recently post-industrialised) economies in which per capita income increases more or less constantly. The second meaning refers to the interdependence of politics and economics in any national state at a particular time (thus one might speak of the 'political economy' of the USA in 1860 and mean the 'balance' of political-cum-economic power held by northern industrial capitalists, southern slave owners and independent small farmers)

Pomeshchik (sing.) pomeshchiki (plural) (Russ.)
until the eighteenth century the holder of land on service tenure; later the
general name for noble landowners

Pomest'e (sing.) pomest'ia (plural) (Russ.)
fiefs; until the eighteenth century, lands held on service tenure; later the
general name for estates owned by noble landowners

Primary/secondary/tertiary employment
the labour force is conventionally divided into a primary sector (agriculture,
fishing, forestry) a secondary sector (manufacturing, building) and a tertiary
sector (services); mining is usually classified as secondary

Primitive accumulation
a Marxist term for the early stage in the development of modern capitalism
when capital was accumulated by violent plunder overseas and the brutal
dispossession of primary producers of their rights to common land

imperialism

Production factors
in classical economic theory, the factors of production are land, labour and
capital (or what Adam Smith called 'stock')

Proto-industrialisation
historians' term for the organisation of manufacturing by merchants who 'put
out' raw materials to handicraft piece workers who produced consumer or
intermediate goods. (Hand-woven cloth sold on to clothing workers to
manufacture would be an intermediate good)

Section/sectional (US)
in American political parlance (and in American historiography) it is
customary to refer to the nation's major geographic regions as 'sections' (the
north east, the mid west, the south, etc.)

Seignior (or seigneur)
lord of the manor; usually refers to a noble entitled to extract labour or money
dues from his serfs and exercise jurisdiction over them

Serfs/ serfdom
agrarian workers obliged to render labour or other dues to their seignior;
system of agricultural production resting on coerced by not slave labour

Slatee (uncertain derivation)
term used throughout West Africa for Muslim slave merchant

Sodomy
anal intercourse with a man, woman or beast (a capital offence in most
Christian jurisdictions until the later nineteenth century)

Terms of trade/net barter terms of trade
economist's term for the relationship between the market value of a country's
exports and the market value of its imports. If, say, a country has to import all
its petroleum oil, and the price of oil suddenly increases four fold without any
compensating adjustment in the market value of its exports, its terms of trade
are said to have deteriorated: it has to sell more abroad to purchase its oil. But
if a country imports all its computers, and the price of imported computers

falls because of technological improvements and productivity gains, without any downward adjustment in the price of its exports, then its terms of trade *improve*. Computers are cheaper, and it can buy more with the same quantity of exports. These simplified examples assume that quantities exchanged across international borders remain the same, while prices change; they are examples of what economists call the 'net barter terms of trade'. Consider, however, the case of the computer-producing country which has made the technological improvements and productivity gains: because it has a competitive advantage in international trade, the quantity of its computer exports increases (perhaps exponentially), so export income rises despite falling unit price. Its 'income terms of trade' have improved. This was roughly the story of Britain's terms of trade during nineteenth industrialisation: productivity gains and technological improvements meant that the unit price of British cotton cloth, pig iron, steel rails, textile machinery and iron ships fell, giving a competitive advantage in international markets; the net barter terms of trade deteriorated, income terms of trade improved.

INDEX